Praise for W

MW00659241

"Chef Keith, a guy from the streets of Detroit, cracked the code to stop the cycle of the ghetto. *Well Done* is an inspiring, entertaining must-read for anyone looking for inspiration and lessons on life."
—Certified Master Chef Edward Janos

"Culinary ambassador is the perfect title for Chef Keith Denard Jones. This versatile culinarian stuns with his kitchen skills presented like art to be viewed and admired before consuming uniquely layered flavors. Beyond the kitchen, he inspires as a spokesperson, encourages as an educator, and shares new skills with consumers. *Well Done* is a great read for anyone who appreciates the passion of a life well-lived through the enjoyment of food."
—Joan Brewster, executive director of American Master Chefs Order

"Chef Keith is the definition of what happens when passion supersedes all other motivations. *Well Done* will give you a taste of his contagious energy and zeal for life as you feel his craving leap from the pages."
—Jim Pike, food-industry executive at Honey Smoked Fish Holdings LLC

"We hire Chef Keith to represent us at major customer events. The unique perspective he brings is such an asset. He has a heart for food, people, and being true to his beliefs. He started as a business associate and became my friend."
—Sarah Hayes, national sales manager for Maritime Products International

"When Chef Keith worked at the prestigious Metropolitan Club, his meticulous planning and attention to details provided members with an exquisite and unrivaled culinary experience. He continues to refine his food expertise as he motivates countless others with his energy, humor, and passion. Chef Keith is the ultimate example and inspiration for extraordinary work ethic and zest for life. Cheers to many more years of your scintillating successes!"
—Dennis and Zachary Meyer, owners of DasMeyerPastry.com

"An insightful story for those of us who enjoy an authentic voice. Chef Keith Jones shares his mouth-watering creations and valuable recipes for success in life. May you delight in his savory excellence."
—Arthur O. Thomas, television and content producer

"Chef Jones is cookin' again. He blended setbacks and challenges with dreams and successes into a harmonizing dish of lessons. Sautéed, simmered, and baked into this marvelously delicious cuisine of wisdom: *Well Done*!"
—Arvell Jones, former creator for DC and Marvel

"Despite the chaos and mayhem in Detroit, Keith inspired, motivated, and influenced me by being a positive role model to pattern my life."
—William Blair Anderson, St. Cloud, MN Chief of Police

"Having known Chef Keith for nearly 50 years, I am amazed at how a kid from Motown became the exceptional chef that he is today. Inspired to feed the masses with international cuisine with soul-food flare, you will experience genuine love in *Well Done*! Bon appétit!"
—Senior Pastor Kenneth James Flowers, Greater New Mt. Moriah M. B. Church in Detroit

Well Done

Bringing Soul to the Recipe of Life

By

Keith Denard Jones

Published by
Queen V Publishing
Englewood, OH
QueenVPublishing.com

Published by
Queen V Publishing
Englewood, OH
QueenVPublishing.com

Library of Congress Catalog Number: 2021909748

ISBN-13: 978-0-9962991-6-9

Edited by Valerie J. Lewis Coleman of Pen of the Writer
PenOfTheWriter.com

Proofread by Ethleen Sawyerr of Speak, Write, Play

Printed in the United States of America

Dedication

I dedicate *Well Done* to a great person, accomplished chef, and dear friend, Claudio Ferrer.

From the moment he flashed a big smile and offered a firm handshake, I knew he was a genuine dude. We had tons of similarities, which strengthened our instant bond. Led by passion and compassion, he was full of life and radiated success. You couldn't help but enjoy being around him.

Far beyond his worldwide culinary achievements, he was willing to help anyone at any time do anything. I marveled at his mastery of personal and professional situations and how he commanded classrooms, kitchens, and cooking demonstrations. Seasoned with humor, he shared his time, knowledge, and experience with up-and-coming chefs and colleagues. If he chose to switch careers, he would easily have been a top-tier comedian.

As a fierce warrior, he worked his plan and adjusted to overcome obstacles. I modeled his never-give-up attitude: no excuses, just determination and perseverance. He had so many endearing qualities that I cannot explain the depth of what he meant to me.

Claudio, thank you for your life, light, and friendship. Your lasting memory and legacy keep you with me. I love you. Rest in peace and power.

Table of Contents

Introduction

My initial motivation for *Well Done* was to guide and encourage those considering the culinary profession. However, like opening wine or fine cheese to breathe and gain full flavor, the more I developed the manuscript, the more character and voice emerged. With an insider look at the industry and corresponding life lessons, this book appeals to anyone entering the workforce, changing professions, or pursuing entrepreneurial success.

Without a dominant male figure to teach me fundamental keys to success, I started with a narrower foundation. I understood what success meant to me, but I didn't have a clue on how to achieve it. Through formal training, informal teachings, and trial-and-error, I peeled back the layers and warmly share my process with you. My goal is summarized in the quote:

> "A wise man learns from his own mistakes. A wiser man learns from the mistakes of others."
> – African proverb

Whatever your journey, my hope is that you find the lesson embedded in every setback and use it to propel you toward your destiny.

Chef Keith Denard Jones
ChefKDJ.com

Keith Denard Jones

Well Done!

As a poor Black kid from Detroit's ghetto, my destiny was pre-determined: the auto plant, military, or prison. I had to break the cycle. So, straight out of high school, I walked into the professional kitchen at Tweeny's Café.

The only thing I knew about food was I enjoyed my mother's and grandmother's cooking. I had to make this culinary thing work. This wasn't just a job; it was my life!

Chef Edward Janos was the first chef to interview me. He only asked two questions: "Do you want to work?" and "Do you want to work hard?" He didn't differentiate due to race, age, or gender. He only saw a kid who expressed a sincere interest in wanting to learn.

As one of only two people of color in the establishment, I felt out of place. I didn't want to make any mistakes or stand out, so I tried to be invisible. Can you do that and succeed in a job? I didn't speak to anyone unless I was spoken to first. I stayed to myself with one goal: make it past 90 days! I had set this arbitrary time limit to determine whether I could earn my place at the culinary table. Every day I felt like I could be terminated, but I had some protection once I hit that 90-day mark.

Even though I was around food all day in my mother's kitchen, this kitchen was different, very different! I was intimidated by everything and everybody. I never felt comfortable. A combination of things unnerved me, but the biggest was my race.

Chef Ed's formal and informal training had tremendous influence on my life. His overpowering intensity resulted in a stressful environment, but it made me a better cook and person. I have countless stories from my first professional kitchen experience. This one comes to mind…

At the end of every shift, we ate a staff meal, a benefit of working there. I politely refused the offer, partly because of my self-imposed timeline, primarily because the kitchen staff processed, handled, and cooked protein and vegetables differently than me.

On my 90-day anniversary, I accepted the meal: filet mignon with green beans and rice pilaf. It took a few minutes to clean my station before I got to the meal that chef prepared. By the time I finished, the filet sat in a puddle of blood. I picked up my plate and went to the chef.

"Hey, there's blood from the steak on my plate. I don't eat it this way. Can you cook this some more for me? I need it well done."

A few members of the kitchen staff overheard me. They shook their heads and laughed.

Chef Ed said, "That steak is cooked perfectly. You are going to eat it the way it was meant to be eaten: a perfect medium-rare."

Shocked and naïve, I said, "Chef, these green beans are too green and hard. I need them to be like they come out of the can."

"Those green beans are perfect, and you'll eat them the way they were meant to be eaten: a perfect al dente."

"Can I have some gravy for my rice?"

Chef moved so close to me that the toes of our shoes touched. He pointed his finger in my face. "If you ever call my sauce 'gravy' again, you'll be fired!"

"Okay." I set the plate on the counter and walked away.

I recovered from the humiliation and developed a beautiful relationship with my mentor. Chef Ed was advancing in the culinary profession with determination that engulfed, overwhelmed, and consumed us. I was mesmerized by him and wanted more. He was a consummate professional, a pro's pro. Perfection was the goal. I had never been around anyone who maintained such high standards. His drive was incredible. Full speed ahead, all the time, but never out of control. He was focused, targeted, and deliberate. He masterfully developed and executed plans. He mastered cooking techniques, building recipes and menus, and developing a team. He worked to attain the title of master chef.

I worked my way from an introductory employee to Chef Ed's right-hand man. I loved to watch him cook on the line. He was organized, fluid, and never wasted motions. The way he prepped items and set up his station was a thing of beauty. I was responsible for the salad station and vegetable prep, but I could watch him for hours. He didn't spend much time in my area because he was too busy. I hurried to set my station and finish prepping to watch him, and indirectly, I learned technique and style. At times, I caught him watching me out of the corner of his eye. He knew what to do to keep me interested, and he played me like a fiddle. We did almost everything in the world of food as he built his name and reputation. I wasn't interested in building my name; I was content with my connection to him.

Chef Ed trained at the prestigious Culinary Institute of America in Hyde Park, New York. He mastered various international cuisines; however, French was his favorite. True to the profession, he taught his staff using books by

Chef Auguste Escoffier, who revolutionized the design and flow of the professional kitchen.[1]

We did things together outside of work, which boosted my loyalty and commitment to him. Like a ferocious pit bull, I put my teeth in him and refused to let go. He came into my life when I needed an influential male figure. My father was an absent alcoholic. My older brother was snatched by street hustlers.

After almost eight years together, Chef Ed kicked me out the nest. He referred me to an interview with Beat Ritchie at the Plaza Club in the Renaissance Center. He was connected to Club Corporations of America (CCA), which owned and managed white tablecloth properties across the United States. With over 250 country clubs, health clubs, and private dining clubs in the company, their annual revenue exceeded a billion dollars.

Ritchie wanted to hire me, but I had one request.

"I'm tired of this snow. I want to relocate somewhere hot."

He confirmed an interview at a CCA property in Phoenix. The sous chef, Chef JI, had accepted a promotion to executive chef in Colorado. He and his manager interviewed me to be his replacement.

About nine months later, Chef JI called me. "Keith, how are you? This is Chef JI."

"Hi, Chef. What can I do for you?"

"I know you interviewed for my sous chef position in Arizona; however, I'd love to have you on my team here in Denver."

---

[1] *A Short Bio of Auguste Escoffier*, EscoffierOnline.com, online: https://www.escoffieronline.com/a-short-bio-of-auguste-escoffier (accessed February 11, 2021).

"Hmm, I don't know."

"I know you had concerns about the weather. I'm from Chicago. I know Detroit winters, and I guarantee that Denver is nothing like it."

I accepted his offer as sous chef for the Metropolitan Club located outside of Denver.

Culinary Notes for Aspiring Chefs

> "If you want to become a great chef, you must work with great chefs. And that's exactly what I did."
> —Chef Gordon Ramsay

A professional kitchen operates using a kitchen brigade, or hierarchy system, which delegates responsibilities to individuals who specialize in certain tasks. For hotels and restaurants with an extensive kitchen staff, the organization is structured as follows:

- Certified master chef is the highest level of certification a chef can receive. The pinnacle of professionalism and skill, this designation is only achieved through the American Culinary Federation.
- Executive chef manages the entire operation.
- Chef de cuisine—chief of the kitchen–oversees operations under guidance of the executive chef.
- Sous chef is known as the deputy, or under chef, who is second in charge and reports to chef de cuisine.
- Saucier, or sauce maker, has one of the most respected positions in the kitchen because many stations were mastered for promotion. This chef is

responsible for sauces, soups, stews, hors d' oeuvres and sautés food to order.

- Chef de partie manages a specific station of line chefs including

Sauté chef	Fish chef	Roast chef
Grill chef	Fry chef	Entrée preparer
Soup chef	Vegetable chef	Pantry chef
Butcher	Pastry chef	
Roundsman (floater)		

Most restaurant kitchens are smaller, so one chef may perform several functions.

Kitchen promotion usually occurs after a candidate masters their current position or station. The executive and sous chefs are notified of the desire for promotion. If the request is accepted, the candidate is required to train their replacement. Ambitious nominees rotate through all positions/stations for elevated knowledge and skills. Attaining executive chef status takes years of practical, hands-on application.

The American Culinary Federation (ACF) offers certifications for sixteen levels of culinarians.[2] Certification combines education, course requirements, work experience, and exams: written and practical. Certified chefs tend to earn more money than non-certified chefs of the same level.

---

[2] *ACF Certification Requirements*, ACFChefs.org, online: https://www.acfchefs.org/download/documents/certify/Certification_Requirements.pdf (accessed February 20, 2021).

Fresh Pasta Dough

Serves 8 to 12

This dish is one of the first things Chef Ed taught me. Although it wasn't my responsibility, he eventually assigned its preparation to me. Fast forward forty years, my wife and I visited him and his wife. He served this fresh pasta Alfredo with house smoked duck as one of the appetizers.

Chef Ed, said, "Keith, do you recognize the pasta?"

"Of course. Five, six, seven."

We enjoyed a hearty laugh. Our wives were clueless to our inside joke.

Note: This recipe requires a pasta maker or pasta roller attachment for stand mixer.

5 cups all-purpose flour
6 large eggs
7 egg yolks
2 teaspoons sea salt

Place the flour on a clean work surface and make a nest. Add the eggs, yolks, and salt to the center. Use a fork to gently break up the eggs, keeping the flour walls intact. Use your hands to gently bring the flour inward to incorporate. Work the dough with your hands to bring it together into a shaggy ball.

Knead the dough for 8 to 10 minutes. At the beginning, the dough should feel dry, but keep kneading until it becomes cohesive and smooth. If the dough still seems too dry, sprinkle your fingers with a tiny bit of water to incorporate. If it's too sticky, dust more flour onto your work surface. Shape the dough into a ball, then wrap in plastic wrap. Let rest at room temperature for 30 minutes.

Dust 4 large baking sheets with flour and set aside.

Slice the dough into four pieces. Gently flatten one into an oval disk. Run the dough through the pasta roller attachment three times on level 1 (the widest setting).

Set the dough piece onto a countertop or work surface. Fold both short ends in to meet in the center, then fold the dough in half to form a rectangle.

Run the dough through the pasta roller three times on level 2, three times on level 3, and one time each on levels 4, 5, and 6.

Lay half of the pasta sheet onto the floured baking sheet and sprinkle with flour before folding the other half on top. Sprinkle more flour on top of the second half. Every side should be floured so that your final pasta noodles don't stick together.

Repeat with remaining dough.

Run the pasta sheets through the pasta roller attachment. Repeat with remaining dough. Cook the pasta in a pot of salted boiling water for 5 to 7 minutes.

Note: Fresh pasta can be stored in the fridge, wrapped in plastic wrap or a Ziploc bag, for up to two days.

Keith Denard Jones

Detroit: From the Streets to Eats

My neighborhood was in inner-city Detroit, filled with negative influences. Most households were headed by single mothers with little structure and children sometimes lacked positive role models. Many of the kids were raised by older siblings or left to fend for themselves. The circumstances jeopardized the likelihood of becoming a productive member of society. I assumed my destiny was predetermined, so I lived it out by going through the motions. If real change was to happen, it had to be a stroke of luck or divine intervention.

The west side—Fenkell and Schoolcraft, Puritan and Greenfield, Grand River and Livernois—was my 'hood. I didn't realize it was the ghetto. The city was tough, and life was hard. But that was my normal. With little money, my mom did her best to provide for us. Of all the things we lacked, love was not one of them. My family and friends and their families showed us genuine love. Since everyone in the neighborhood lived hand-to-mouth, we rallied together to help each other. No reason to be ashamed or embarrassed, just keep the kids out of harm's way.

The city taught me lessons I wouldn't have learned anywhere else. The older I got, the more I experienced the differences of the people in other neighborhoods. I understood whom to trust, where to go, and where to avoid. Survival instincts. The life was fast and intense. The lessons could be astounding or, God forbid, deadly, but that's how I lived. I have battle scars, memories, nightmares, and closeted skeletons, but I also have knowledge, wisdom, and experience for having lived through it.

All of us neighborhood kids should've been in school, taking the safe and legitimate route, but that required commitment, hard work, and dedication. I was on the safe path, but my return on investment wouldn't come until many years later. Drug dealers used kids to distribute, so they would take the fall if caught.

The allure of fast money and all its benefits was too much for many of my peers, so they bought into the hype of money, power, and respect! Although misguided, they developed business acumen, crafting plans to generate revenue and streamline costs.

My mother retired from the plant years ago, and my sister and brother made their living there. The only thing I knew about the military was that I had to be ready, willing, and able to follow orders. I was way too cool for that.

About one week before I left for Denver, I said goodbye to friends and relatives who tried to make it a happy affair. My immediate family didn't offer any fanfare or celebration. Their somberness felt like I was going to the penitentiary.

My hardest goodbye was to my girl—my high school sweetheart. After seven years of dating, I asked her to marry me. Both from broken homes, we committed to young love, school, and working toward a better future.

I went into the kitchen, and she went into the office; it was the beginning of the end. My fledging career didn't afford me the luxuries of confidence, pockets full of money, and tons of free time to woo my girl. Too immature to realize that "stuff" didn't impress her, I ran away from her and straight into work! I worked long hours, late nights, weekends, and holidays to make more money. She wanted me, not a workaholic. The relationship deteriorated, leaving broken promises and unfulfilled dreams. Collateral damage. The kitchen became my master. I created a perfect storm, which swept her and our nine-year relationship away.

I took my time packing my clothes and small belongings into boxes. I was leaving the only home I'd ever known, Detroit, to start a new life in Denver.

Unsure about what to expect, I was excited and scared at the same time. I would be the first from my family to leave Michigan, so I didn't have anyone to ask for advice. I was leaving my family, my girl, and my friends for what? A small chance at something? A long shot? I didn't know. A rumble churned in my stomach. Whether nerves, fear, or anticipation, I had accepted the position. Turning back was not an option.

Mom's Macaroni and Cheese

Serves 12

I was the child who stopped playing outside with friends to help my mother in the kitchen. Sunday dinners were the best because she prepared mega meals to have leftovers for the week, and I was her little line chef.

When I moved away from home, I was homesick. I missed my mother's cooking, so I made her macaroni and cheese for my first solo Thanksgiving. Her dish has been a staple on my holiday table ever since. It's a family favorite that gets me a little closer to home.

1 lb. elbow macaroni pasta
¼ cup butter
¼ cup all-purpose flour
1 tablespoon + 1 teaspoon salt
⅛ teaspoon ground white pepper
1 cup chicken or vegetable stock
2 cups milk
3 cups sharp cheddar cheese shredded

Preheat oven to 400°F.

Add 1 tablespoon salt to a large pot of water. Bring to boil. Add pasta, stirring occasionally for 8 minutes or until pasta is al dente (chewy and firm). Remove from water and drain well.

In a large saucepan, melt butter over medium-high heat. Once it begins to foam, add flour. Cook for 3 to 4 minutes or until it begins to turn pale yellow. Whisk in chicken stock, whipping constantly until smooth. Add milk, 1 teaspoon of salt and white pepper. Continue to whip. Bring the sauce to a simmer. Reduce heat to medium-low. Cook out sauce, whipping occasionally for another 8 to 10 minutes. The sauce will thicken. Turn off heat. Add 2 cups of shredded cheddar cheese. Stir until melted and combined.

Transfer the cooked macaroni into a casserole dish, then pour in cheese sauce. Stir to thoroughly combine pasta and sauce. Sprinkle remaining cup of shredded cheddar cheese on top of casserole. Bake in preheated oven for 20 to 30 minutes or until the top is golden brown. Remove from oven. Serve immediately.

Colorado, Here I Come

I have no idea why I chose Colorado. I hadn't visited many states and never lived on my own. But, with one calculated decision, I took care of both.

What would this new life bring? Will I like my job? Will my coworkers like me? Can I make this work, or will I have to return home with my tail tucked between my legs?

My mother didn't want her baby to leave home, but she was a saint about it—positive and supportive. She only had two requests: don't make the drive alone and don't drive straight through.

The second request was easy. I'd find a hotel at the midpoint for a one-night stay. Finding a travel buddy proved to be more difficult. The only people I thought would go were immediate family. But, because I struggled with leaving, I couldn't bear extending the goodbye a few more days.

My mother suggested my father. Short on options, I considered him…for a millisecond.

He wasn't much of a father. Some may even label him a sperm donor. He was a violent drunk who let alcohol destroy his life and damage those around him. His rage resulted in fights, arrests, and frequent hospital visits. He blacked out without remembering anything from his violent episodes.

Along with my mother and older siblings, LaGreta and Roger, we weaved our lives around his destruction. His behavior took us from potential to poverty. We weren't blessed with money, so we didn't have many options.

Counseling? Please! We did just enough to scrape by, so paid professional help was a luxury we could not afford. As adults, my siblings and I made our peace with him.

Embedded in every experience is a valuable life lesson. He taught me what not to do. One prominent lesson happened when I was about ten years old. I asked LaGreta—who was thirteen during the incident—to provide her version to offset my fuzzy memory.

> Late one afternoon, my mom, my brother, Keith, and I sat at the dinner table. Like so many other times, my father came home drunk. His perpetual anger on red alert, he went after my mother. They argued.
>
> He seemed madder than usual. He yelled, cursed, and pulled the phone off the wall. He picked up a plate of food, threw it out the back door, and then jumped on my mom. He held her in a pseudo headlock and drug her around the room as he broke windows in the breakfast nook.
>
> With fear and rage, I cried, "Leave my mother alone! Stop!"
>
> He picked up a can of corn from the counter and hurled it at me. It struck the left side of my head. Blood trickled from the gash.
>
> I believe he shocked himself because he released his grip.
>
> Like a protective mother hen, Mom gathered us so we could get out of there. I think my brother, Roger, came in at the end of this situation because he had been outside

> riding his bike. Keith locked himself in the bathroom.
>
> Once Dad realized we were leaving, he flew into another rage. "Whatever you want, you better take it with you!"
>
> We left with only the clothes on our backs and stayed the night with a family friend.
>
> When Mom returned the next day, Dad was passed out in a pile of rubble. He broke everything in the house with a baseball bat and shredded our clothes.
>
> He woke with no memory of what he did. Devastating.

No way was I riding halfway across the country with that loser, so I dug deep into my Rolodex. After a couple days of begging and negotiating, my friend, Gerald Rucker, agreed to ride with me. I promised to purchase a one-way plane ticket back to Detroit and buy his food. What a small price to pay for such a kind gesture.

My girlfriend's father was into CB radios. He had an awesome system in his basement and a nationwide reputation to go with it. His powerful system disrupted, interrupted, or damaged his neighbors' radios and TV signals. He had regular visits and fines from the FCC. His handle was Fu Manchu. I enjoyed watching him do his thing.

For the upcoming drive, he gave me a system for safety purposes. He taught me how to work it, explaining that many people used CB radios to stay awake while driving.

I was excited to play with the CB. Getting to the job became secondary. We had plenty of fun getting into heated discussions and arguments with truckers. We had no knowledge of etiquette, only curse words and venom for whoever cared to listen.

We were in Nebraska before we realized that it wasn't a good idea to let people know we were traveling west on I-80 in a burgundy-and-silver Honda Accord with Michigan license plates. We put a bullseye on our backs: two black guys driving a foreign car through America. How stupid were we?

The trip was almost 1,300 miles. At 65 mph, that's twenty hours of boring driving through Michigan, Indiana, Illinois, Iowa, and Nebraska.

To keep the second promise to my mother, we stayed the night in the Cornhusker State. Trucks and tractors everywhere, but no Black folks anywhere.

"Hey, Dorothy. You're not in Kansas anymore!"

Oven-Roasted Filet Mignon with Truffle Demi-Glace

Serves 4

As the chef of a members-only club, I had to learn how to cook several staples including this steak. I wanted to prepare more cutting-edge cuisine; however, my general manager made sure my foundation was solid first. Great lesson: learn how to satisfy your clientele.

Filet Mignons
4 6-ounce filet mignons, center cut
Kosher salt and freshly ground black pepper to taste
2 tablespoons olive oil
3 tablespoons butter
1 clove garlic, thinly sliced
2 sprigs fresh thyme

Twenty minutes before they're to be cooked, remove filets from refrigerator to come to room temperature (about 68-72°F).

Preheat oven to 300°F.

Season each filet with salt and pepper. Over high heat, heat 2 tablespoons olive oil in a large heavy-bottomed skillet. Sear filets until brown and crispy, about 3 minutes per side. Turn heat to low. Add 3 tablespoons butter, sliced garlic and 2 sprigs thyme. Using a spoon, baste the filets with the butter. Put pan in preheated oven. Cook 5-6 minutes for medium rare or until an internal temperature thermometer reads 130°F. If you want to ruin a great steak, cook it longer! Rest filets 5 minutes. Pour truffle demi-glace on the plate, then place the filet on top.

Truffle Demi-Glace

2 tablespoons olive oil
2 medium-sized Portobello mushrooms
2 medium shallots, minced
1 small garlic clove, minced
1 cup brandy
1 quart demi-glace
2 sprigs fresh thyme
2 tablespoons butter
Kosher salt and pepper to taste
1 ounce truffle pieces
2 tablespoons fresh basil, chiffonade

Preheat saucepan with 2 tablespoons olive oil. Separate stems from mushrooms. Scrape the underside to remove gills. Chop mushrooms and stems. Place in preheated saucepan. Add shallots and garlic. Sauté until it softens and the mushrooms deliver their liquid. Deglaze the pan with brandy. **Note: Be careful because it could flame.** Add demi-glace and thyme. Cook over low heat until it reduces to sauce consistency. Strain through a fine mesh strainer. Add butter and season with salt. Add truffle pieces and fresh basil.

Denver: Failure is Not an Option

We arrived in Denver on Friday, October 10, 1986 at 3:36 PM MST. I was scheduled to start work Monday at 8:00 AM. I drove to the job and looked in the area for my new "home." It didn't take long to find a nice one-bedroom apartment. I had a small issue: no bed. I purchased a sleeping bag, pad, pillow, and boom box to hold me over until my belongings arrived.

Denver was a big adjustment, especially because the pace was much slower than Detroit. Out here all alone, I was happy with my workaholic lifestyle; the vicious cycle I had packed along with my belongings. My job and this profession can be demanding, so work became my sanctuary.

When things weren't going right in my personal life, I threw myself into work where everything made sense. Issues with my lady, bills, the car? No problem. Let me get to work early and stay late. My escape focused on two things: keeping my job and being the best that I could be. I wasn't smart enough to be scared, only naïve leaving what I knew behind to make a go of it here.

Chef JI was professionally trained at The Culinary Institute of America. I was classically trained by Master Chef Ed. My official title was sous-chef. For us to be successful, we had to get along to develop a solid team. As I learned from Chef Ed, you cannot do everything yourself. You are only as good as your crew.

Our unofficial titles of "bad cop" and "good cop" were based on his rules-regulations-and-procedures management style, while I focused on making great food. My boss, who had knowledge of teamwork, lacked firsthand experience to apply it. Instead of exciting and motivating the staff, he had the opposite effect. I knew he would be the biggest obstacle to my success.

I became skilled at building a team, leading, and optimizing every staff member. On an on-going basis, I assessed them for key roles of team leader, sauté/line cook, broiler person, pantry person, pastry person, and banquet staff. It didn't take me long to turn my crew into a team!

Our club wasn't large, nor did we have enough volume for dedicated staff. So team members had multiple tasks. We were cross-trained and helped each other with the rush of new orders and banquet business.

The private dining facility, The Metropolitan Club, was inside Denver Tech Center, which was located in an affluent part of town. Over 16,000 square feet, each of the five service rooms, which sat 30 to 150 guests, had a different theme. The main dining room had a strict jacket-and-tie dress code and lavish decor imported from Italy. The bathrooms were out of this world, something to behold.

We had one of the most luxurious properties in the state. The membership roster consisted of the who's who of metro Denver: politicians, doctors, lawyers, entrepreneurs, bankers, and sports and local celebrities. These fine trappings and exclusive clientele gave us freedom and flexibility to be out in front of the culinary scene. Trendsetters! We had to manage costs and quality. We could do anything we wanted if we could justify the investment. The sell was easy because all we had to do was say, "The members asked for it." We had everything we needed to make it work. I had a beautiful run as executive chef for over nine years.

We needed to get our core players. The club had an excellent reputation, so finding people wasn't a problem. Turning them into the best team took time. Although I anticipated resistance from the team—change isn't always fun—my boss, the executive chef, was the biggest obstacle.

The manager, chef, and club were on the hook for my relocation expenses, and I knew they were looking to get their money's worth.

One December evening, we were extremely busy. Every seat in the house was occupied, parties were on top of one another in private rooms, and á la carte dining had sold out. We were winding down from the high of exceeding expectations and overwhelming **all** our guests.

I was called into the manager's office. I got a sick feeling in my stomach. I thought, *Why does he want to talk to me?*

When I walked in the office, the executive chef was there. "Hey, what's up?"

Oblivious to his motives and pumped from a great night, the heavy tension caused my stomach to explode.

The manager said, "Keith, what were you responsible for tonight?"

"I was responsible for everything in the club except the Board of Directors Dinner."

The Board of Directors Dinner was the club's opportunity to thank them for their service. Members came with spouses or significant others for a luxury dining experience. Everything for the annual tradition was first class and at the club's expense. I set up the chef with the menu from hors d'oeuvres through dessert. The only thing he had to do was execute it, making sure it went smoothly. Because I knew how important the dinner was, I assigned a couple of key kitchen staff to help.

I took the remaining staff to manage the rest of the business. Like an orchestra conductor, I lead the kitchen and expedited service. I made sure everyone hit their required notes with precision. The night was magical for the crew and me.

With minimal hands-on application, Chef JI had to operate outside his proverbial box. I set him up for success and hoped that he would do well, but deep down inside I had doubts. His dinner service was a disaster: undercooked food, hot food served cold, and courses took way too long.

"Just as I suspected." He ripped into the chef using choice words. "You don't work at this club anymore! You can either sign this resignation letter," he slid the document across the table, "and we'll relocate you to another property within our family, or you can go out on your own and do whatever you want. The choice is yours." Within a year, the executive chef had worn out his welcome. The manager looked at me. "Congratulations. You're my new executive chef, and you're running this club now! Review this compensation package and we'll discuss it later."

I sat with my mouth open.

He looked at Chef JI. "I need your answer before you leave this room." He looked back at me. "Do you have any questions?"

"No, sir."

"Please give me the chance to tell the staff. You may be excused."

I still wonder if the chef thought I had something to do with his dismissal. Did he think I sabotaged him to get his position? I just did my job, but doubt remains.

I had gained the respect of the management and staff. They counted on me to deliver a great experience on each visit. The general manager appreciated me and expressed how much I meant to the overall success of the club. I was a team player, the MVP. What an incredible feeling. Success and respect were intoxicating; the more I got, the more I wanted. Uh oh. There's that cycle again!

I developed a great team, easily hitting 85% efficiency daily. After a few years, we ran into a problem: little to no room for promotions. My staff was happy to stay with me, seemingly forever, but I wanted to reward them with more money. I moved one of them to another property so that everyone else could get a little raise. I promoted a few of my sous chefs to executive chefs. They got their own properties to oversee. I was promoted to regional executive chef and, with four colleagues, we controlled all the properties from Colorado westward. I was still a workaholic with dividends paid in money, power, notoriety, and respect. It took me back to the days of watching young street men with their fast money, except I earned it with honest, hard work.

In the midst of learning my craft and climbing the proverbial ladder of success, I found love. About two years into working in Denver, I met and married Martha Kemp. Somehow during my hectic culinary life, we managed to blend our families.

Call me a polygamist because I had two wives: Martha and my job. I made many sacrifices—some intentional, others not—to keep the accolades coming. The unrelenting work has no concern for you or your personal life. The perpetual fast-paced life was complicated by the fact that if you didn't take an opportunity, a comparable replacement was ready and willing.

When a chef asked you to do *anything*, the answer was always, "Yes, chef!" This assertion often led to more opportunities that were great for career success. However, it creeps into your personal life and throws you out of balance.

Instead of enjoying life, I focused on keeping my job, learning, and earning more money. To increase my value, I had to learn more, which meant spending more time at work. A vicious cycle!

Almost everyone strives to be their absolute best in this competitive business. However, many chefs assume that they're competing against other chefs. In reality, a chef is only in competition with him or herself.

"Best" is subjective; however, money is a major factor in ranking. If your club was cash poor, you couldn't do much. If your club had cash and a healthy membership, you could get the finer things like staff, equipment, and décor, which helped enhance its reputation.

Pertaining to money, our club was in the middle of the 260 clubs in the corporation, but we had more HEART. I was fully committed and demanded the same from my staff. Visitors from all over the country recognized us as one of the best properties within the company. With every member interaction, meal served, and event hosted, I was proud to be the executive chef. We built a family atmosphere.

Much happened during my nine-year tenure, but three incidents stand out. I often reflect on them as valuable life lessons.

1. My promotion to regional executive chef
2. My resignation from regional executive chef
3. My interview with a local magazine

The organizational structure of CCA mandated that the executive chef had two bosses: a direct club manager and an indirect regional chef. I spent every day with the manager, which allowed us to learn and grow. We built an excellent relationship personally and professionally. To this day, I love and respect him. The regional chef was a different story. He was executive chef of his own club in Oakland, California and had the added responsibility of about fifty properties in our region. He traveled extensively, visiting each club three to five times a year. His main purpose was to ensure adherence to corporate standards, excellent food preparation, financials aligned with projections, and executive chefs actively trained sous chefs to become executive chefs for other company properties. Since CCA was in ongoing negotiations to purchase or manage new properties, we needed a steady flow of trained, ready individuals. In case of an emergency, the regional chef served as a replacement chef.

He provided extra assurance and incentive to club managers and chefs to do a good job. His solution to any problem was effective: immediate replacement of the problem child. He convinced his superiors to let him form a Regional Chef team. Four chefs and I gave the company options and flexibility in dealing with club issues or problem chefs.

When we first met, the nicest thing the regional chef said to me was "hello." Everything that followed was a ream session.

"You call yourself a chef. Look at the filth in these hoods! You call yourself a chef? Look at the dirt on the ceiling and ceiling fan! You call yourself a chef? Look at your lettuce mix. I see wilted lettuce! You call yourself a chef?"

I did not like this man, but I couldn't do anything about it. His criticisms were right and fair, but his delivery pissed me off.

He got more calls than anyone I had ever met and spent most of his visits with the manager or on his phone. Although his visits with me were brief, the agonizing time together seemed like hours. Seldom did he say anything kind. He spewed biting criticisms of everything I did, which I took personally. After every visit, I was ready to fight.

I thought, *Forget this job! We can take this matter outside. I'll show you wilted lettuce!*

Every time I saw him, I feared I was losing my job. Most of his visits were scheduled, but the unannounced ones were a pain far worse than any health inspector. I knew he was going to chew my butt, tell me how much I sucked, and threaten my job. The manager and I picked up shards of shattered confidences when he left.

To maintain our elite club status, my manager requested cutting-edge food. I created seasonal and daily-specials menus, which included exotic products. The more exotic, the more expensive to purchase and ship. When my food-cost calculations exceeded the company max, the manager and I determined a price and ran with the new dish.

Because of the two-tier supervisor model, I needed the regional chef's approval. I handed him my proposed menu with the exotic foods.

"Specials are never to exceed the $40 price point. This menu is no good."

Since the manager had already approved the menu, I implemented it anyway. The staff loved the changes and so did the members. The unique dining experience exhibiting the latest trends and the hottest food in the culinary world was another notch in the club's belt.

During an unannounced visit, the regional chef saw the specials and elevated pricing. He got with me in front of my team.

"Hey, Keith. I told you not to go over $40 on your specials. I see you didn't listen. You disobeyed a direct order."

I chose culinary to avoid the harsh directives of military officers.

He got in my face, waving menus around like a mad man.

Concerned about my employment status, I debated with the angel and devil sitting on my shoulders. Do I humbly leave, or do I give him a piece of my mind? Should I bite my tongue and beg for forgiveness, or fire back and burn the bridge? It took me a moment to regain my composure because my first instinct was attack. *Since I'm going to lose my job anyway, I might as well give him a piece of my mind!*

I stepped inches from his face. "You might be right calling me out on the price, but you do not sign my paycheck. The manager does, and he's the one who told me to do it! If you have a problem, talk to him. Furthermore, I do not appreciate you breaking my balls over this or that. I don't like the way you talk to me with that smug, condescending attitude. You think you're better than me? If you want to fire me, then do what you gotta do. I'm not taking your crap anymore." As I unloaded, I got more fired up. By the time I was done, I was prepared to step outside and settle this matter like men. I rope-a-doped in my mind with virtual fists at the ready. Job? What job? This was personal.

He looked at me for what seemed like forever. "I'm glad you finally said something and stood up for yourself. I wondered what was taking you so long." He extended his hand. "I'd like for you to join my team. I want to promote you to regional chef. Now that I know you have it in you, I'm sure you'll be able to handle yourself and the chefs you'll manage."

What in the world? I went from losing my job to a promotion and more money. Life is funny.

The regional chef taught me how to be a better professional, leader, and boss. He showed me how to step outside my food world, expand my vision, and focus on the bigger picture. He knew I had the skills, but he needed to bring them out of me. Well done!

Resignation from the executive chef position was the second momentous pivot in my career. For about eighteen months, I was the golden child who could do no wrong. That is, until the company asked me to relocate to another part of the country.

The western regional manager offered to promote me to a larger club in the Pacific Northwest. I could keep my regional chef status and earn more money. They agreed to pay my relocation expenses and thirteen months of rent or mortgage, whichever was cheaper.

I liked everything except for the rent/mortgage offer. Denver's real estate market was upside down. Buyers could choose from tons of properties. The few houses that did sell had to slash the asking price. If that happened to me, I would lose money. In this win-lose scenario, I was the loser.

"How about you buy my house and take that unknown variable out of the equation?"

"No can do."

"You sure?" I was up for the move, but not at the risk of financial ruin.

"Yeah, I'm sure."

"Then I have to decline your offer."

Career suicide.

My manager worked out a deal to move closer to his mother-in-law who had health issues. Almost overnight, the new manager, whom I will refer to as "MJ" for Manager John, was on the scene for what management called "a smooth transition."

MJ was a straight-faced company man who had the personality of a wood plank. He never smiled or had personal conversations. He had no backbone, especially when it came to dealing with the club's Board of Directors and his superiors. Every good leader knows that sometimes you must go to battle for your people. The previous manager understood this concept, which made us stronger and united as a family. MJ was a joke! Whatever he was told to do, he did regardless of the results.

He was quiet, sneaky, and not to be trusted. The Detroit streets taught me that.

Our battle started week one when he said that he was changing our standing meeting time from Thursday at 3 PM to 8 AM.

When I found out, I went to him. "Hey, MJ. I have a conflict with this change. I won't be able to make it."

"As a department head, you are expected to be at all staff meetings. Work out the conflict."

"I can't." I walked my daughters to the bus stop and waited with them until the bus arrived at 8:05 AM. We had a ball during our brief time together. No way was I changing our morning ritual for this inconsiderate jerk. "I will not be there."

"No is not an option."

For two months, he had the early meeting. And for two months, I did my family thing. One morning, I got to work at about 9 AM. He wanted to write me up for insubordination. Absolutely not! How could I go from being honored corporate-wide to written up? Are you kidding me?

A month later, he changed the meeting back to 3 PM, but it was too late. The damage had been done. I came to work ready to do my job and looking for a fight. My job shifted from something I loved to one I hated. My frustration was compounded as I still spent lots of time there because I owed it to my staff to lead by example. They saw the volatile situation unfold. Since MJ was intimidated by me, he thundered his vengeance on my team. On the few occasions I wasn't there to protect them, he was downright mean.

He called me to his office for a reprimand.

He looked at papers spread on his desk. "Keith, your food costs are too high."

"No way are my numbers off. Let me investigate and get back to you." It didn't take long to discover that this low-down snake had changed prices on menus filed at the corporate office. He ran **two** sets of prices and numbers, which is illegal and unethical.

I called him on it. "I found out what's wrong. The menus at the corporate office are priced differently than the menus here. Once you run the numbers with the proper pricing, all my numbers are spot on."

With an inquisitive look, he said, "I don't know how or who could've changed those prices."

Since he and I were the only people authorized to do anything with pricing, I knew he was the culprit.

He tried to flip the script on me and put me in hot water with corporate. No telling what he said about me behind my back.

I unleashed a little 'hood on him. "You don't want to screw with me. You're trying to take food out of my family's mouths! I'll play the race card on you so fast your head will spin! You want a piece of me? Bring it! I have almost ten years of decorated service. And six months with you, I suck? Don't think so. Not today, not ever!" I stormed out of his office, cleared my locker, and exited the building.

After a one-day, self-imposed cooling period, I returned to work as if everything was great. I was satisfied having set the boundary for how to be treated.

We rarely spoke or looked at one another. His negative aura and terrible leadership created a hostile workplace. I drew my line in the sand, and he couldn't do anything without severe repercussions from the company. If anyone were to leave, it should be him; but I knew that it was over for me. I had to move on, so I contacted my former manager for advice.

"Do not burn your bridge no matter how badly you want to. Find another job." He was a member of Club Managers Association. He offered to make a few calls to help me. "Do your best to leave your position and club better than when you started so that you walk out the door on top."

I didn't want just any job. I was making good money and had goals to accomplish. Only two places in the metro area could afford me, but those jobs were not available. Just my luck. It took me less than a week to find an executive chef position at a private country club with a nice manager. After I accepted, I informed MJ of my pending departure.

"Can we speak in private?"

We walked to his office. He sat at the desk and wrung his hands together.

Not that I'm an imposing figure, but he was afraid to be around me. From a standing position, I said, "I'm turning in my two-week notice." I walked out. Oh, what a great feeling!

As soon as my staff got word of me leaving, many of them turned in quit notices. I was moved by their gesture of loyalty. As good-hearted people and amazing employees, all eight members of my core group found gainful employment. My sous chef left the culinary profession to work in construction. Wow!

What a tremendous life lesson: never let anyone have that type of influence over you. Challenges, obstacles, and haters will come into your life with the sole purpose of distracting you from achieving your goals. Determination, integrity, humility, and belief in yourself must be mastered for success on your journey.

What goes around, comes around. And it didn't take long for MJ to get his. He ran the club right into the ground in just a few months. By the time the members caught on to his inadequacies, it was too late. The momentum of the downward spiral he created disrupted the club and parent company. They couldn't recover. Within a couple of years, CCA sold the club to the members, who soon realized how difficult it was to manage. They decided to shut the doors and cut their losses. Without fanfare or celebration, the club closed and faded like it never existed.

I hadn't worked at a country club or any place where food wasn't the main draw. I accepted the job at the Lakewood Country Club and had a nice two-year run. MC, the manager, was next in line to operate a property that I wanted. I figured connecting with him at this property positioned me to go with him when he transferred to the next one. I took a significant cut in pay, but the potential reward was worth the risk.

The general manager was a nice, athletically built, and attractive man. He had great rapport with the members and knew the business.

When a chef takes on a new property, three major challenges must be addressed upfront:

1. The food
2. The staff
3. The numbers, including monitoring and controlling costs for food and labor

It didn't take me long to make an impression. Knowing that a chef is only as good as his/her team, I started there. My team was pretty good, so I only made a couple of staffing adjustments. Overhauling attitude and company culture were challenges for me because food didn't rule, golf did!

Upon my arrival, food and beverage were necessary evils to which they did not commit. No cohesion existed between the food and beverage and golf departments, membership, and management. Everyone seemed to be in it for themselves.

I knew the management team largely influenced the success or failure of a club. I had to get them on my side. I wore my passion on my sleeve and wanted them to understand that food and beverage was just as important as golf.

Many of the manager's decisions favored golf, which I took as a personal insult. After several occasions of being on the wrong side, I decided that I needed allies. With the help of the manager, I developed the social side of the club and a core group of members who went to bat on my behalf. Yes, I had my own groupies. It was nice to have that pendulum swing in my favor on member matters. I decided to stick my head so far up the golf department's butt until I tickled their tonsils. I worked both sides of the fence, and it felt good.

I changed the direction and culture of the culinary department while increasing enthusiasm of members and staff. I wanted them to know that we made great food and cared about every dish. Be it a staff meal or something ordered off the menu, I settled for nothing less than perfection. The staff depended on me to deliver a high-quality food experience. That's not to say that we didn't have issues along the way; most were member interactions.

Late one evening, we concluded a busy food service night of á la carte dining, private parties, and a special event. Such hectic nights became standard once we were recognized as a food destination. I made the last pass through the dining room to make sure guests' food, services, and overall experiences met or exceeded expectations. I was decked out in my crisp, clean uniform, complete with a tall chef's hat and polished clogs. I dressed to impress because it was a status thing to have the chef come to your table and talk about your dining experience.

As I worked the dining room, an intoxicated guest said something to me.

Because his words slurred, I didn't understand him. "Excuse me?" I walked toward to his table.

He muttered.

Given the great run we just finished, I expected another rave review. I moved closer to him. "Excuse me, sir. I couldn't quite hear you."

In a louder volume, he said, "Hey, nigger. You think you're hot stuff? Your food sucks!"

I heard him and several other people did, too. Stunned.

While I gathered myself, his wife stood.

She jumped in front of him. "Oh, please don't mind him. He's drunk."

In my mind, I had beat his tail. He was an older gentleman who would have been an easy win. I wanted to go after him, but I could not afford to lose my excellent reputation or job. The culinary business is small, especially in the private/country club segment. If I had done anything of note, it would've spread like wildfire throughout the community. I chose to smile like I didn't hear him and visited more guests.

I returned to the kitchen furious. I paced. I had been called that name before, but never in a professional setting.

His wife came into the kitchen to apologize for her husband's behavior.

"No problem." I walked to a private room which had to be reset for the next day's activities.

She followed me, making nice conversation and apologizing. She was one of my original groupies. We had done a number of social events together, all of which were well-received by members.

We stood outside the banquet room when her husband walked up and spewed his foulness toward me. "Hey, nigger. You think you're hot stuff? Your food sucks!"

Adrenaline rose and blood raced through my veins, but I remained calm. I glared at him. "I'm about to take off my hat, which means I'm not on the clock." I took off my hat, popped it in the air, and set it on a table. "Say that to me again and I'll bust your butt." I took a fighter's stance and leaned back ready to swing at him.

His wife jumped between us, pushing him back and almost shoving him to the floor. She looked at me and apologized profusely, but it didn't register.

"No one talks to me like that. Screw him, this job, and everything else."

"He's an old harmless man who wouldn't hurt anyone."

"I do not give a care. I'm ready to go." I bounced back-and-forth on the balls of my feet.

She pushed him into the dining room, yapping all the way. I don't think it registered with him, but it felt good to hear her stand up for me.

I stayed at the club for about another year. He never spoke to me again; however, his wife remained one of my biggest supporters. And we're still friends to this day.

Another significant incident happened with my good friend and greatest supporter. Bobby was the service director and excellent at his job. He knew his food, wine, and people. He was hands-on in every aspect, making sure he took care of members and his staff. He had a pleasant, outgoing personality. He became my go-to guy for pretty much every situation I incurred at the club. Also a workaholic, between the two of us, no detail in food and beverage was missed.

Bobby was an attractive Hispanic man with jet-black hair, dark olive skin, and hazel brown eyes. He stood about 5'10" and looked like a cross between Ricky Ricardo and Caesar Romero. He was always well-dressed with the right accents: bracelet, necklace, ring.

Our working relationship developed into a friendship and eventually a business venture. He knew the front-end—staff, service, buffet design—while I knew food. We became quite the team. Our hustle grew into a thriving catering business, providing nice, steady income.

Bobby had developments in his personal life—marriage and buying a bar. Over time, he abused the privilege of bar ownership and drank way too much. This habit led to him wanting something stronger. He turned to substances, which took over his life. He destroyed most of his friendships and his marriage.

I called him multiple times to team with me on an outside catering event. He was nowhere to be found. Since I wasn't going to do the event without him, I walked away from it. Two weeks later, I found out that he was locked up for double murder for killing his ex-wife and her lover.

Shocked to my core, I couldn't understand how someone who had so much could throw it all away. I doubt I'll ever get over it. I tried to learn from his mistakes. Life is precious. Things can change in an instant, so strive to do your absolute best and make the most of every second.

By design, I spent a couple of years at this club. My plan to get to the high-end private club was working. Well, until the manager turned down the job offer! Just like that, my plan fell apart. The valuable lesson: nothing compares to having your own!

I knew my time with him was short, so I looked for another job. Without much effort, I found one at a different high-end private country club. I had achieved the ultimate job with prestige, a strong, financially-stable membership, and a fantastic salary. It almost seemed too good to be true.

I had a "golden handcuff" job where management's philosophy of we'll-pay-you-this-huge-salary-but-WE-OWN-YOU prevailed. They were upfront about it, so I knew what I was getting into. But I hated it. They dictated what I did and how. The groupthink culture diminished my creativity and passion. The employees walked around like zombies waiting for the general manager (GM) to give instructions for the day. What a shame.

I had never experienced anything like this and didn't know how to handle it. Engulfed by the disease, I felt sick anytime I was presented with a decision. What I wanted seldom aligned with the catatonic mindset of management. I felt unappreciated, undervalued, and uneasy.

Although I did my best, the GM stayed on me.

At least five times a day, he said, "Keith, that's not the way we do this or that. We want you to be more like us." It seemed like his job was to change me.

I tried to have meetings with the rest of the management team, but they looked at me like I was crazy. No matter where I went or what I did, he was there peering at me. I needed the money, so I kept my peace and took the disrespect.

I supervised a line cook with a history of problems that hadn't been documented. Club management asserted that he was an alcoholic who wandered in hours late, sometimes too hungover to work. They wanted him gone, and they wanted me to do it. They suggested that I start the process of terminating him. I was charged to "make it clean without any fear that he could sue us."

Because I had not witnessed this undocumented behavior, I said, "As far as I'm concerned, his slate is clean. If he does his job, then he won't have any issues with me."

In the three months I worked there, the line cook, whom I'll refer to as "Mr. J." was the model employee: timely, considerate, and respectful. He worked from 7 AM to 4 PM in his company issued uniform.

Mr. J scheduled a paid day off. He came to the job to get his paycheck from me.

"Good morning, chef. Can I have my check?" He wore skintight blue jeans. The leather belt had a huge western motif buckle polished to the nines. His snakeskin boots looked authentic. He finished the ensemble with a long-sleeve western shirt, bolo tie, and an oversized wide-brimmed hat.

I looked him up and down. "Holy smokes, Mr. J. I had no idea you were a cowboy!"

With a slight grin, he said, "This is typical for me when I'm not at work."

I chuckled. "Let me see if the checks are ready." I returned a few minutes later with Mr. J.'s check.

The assistant manager, Mr. N., came from behind a tall artificial tree. He called me into my office.

"Chef, you can't talk to your employees that way even if they're not scheduled to work."

"Talk to him what way? What did I say?"

"You called him a cowboy, which sounds like you have something against cowboys."

"Really? You're kidding, right? He *was* dressed like a cowboy! I'm not making anything of it, just stating the obvious." The aha-you-hired-me-to-fire-him-for-his-alternative-lifestyle lightbulb flashed. "Aside from that, you can't tell me how to talk to my employees."

"I most definitely can and will. You all work for me!"

"Hold on. I didn't say anything wrong and don't need approval from you to talk to my employees. That's not why I was hired! Now I have a problem with you thinking you can control me." My mind raced. I got angrier when I realized they tried to use me to do their dirty work.

He gave a smug boy-I-own-you-and-we-both-know-it glare.

"Mr. N, you do not own me." I paused for emphasis. "As a matter of fact, I don't want to work here anymore. How much time do you need?"

"Excuse me?"

I looked at him to ensure he read my lips and heard my words. "You heard me. How much time do you need?"

"You can leave right now!"

I grabbed a few personal things and headed for the door. On my way out, I asked my sous chef to collect the rest of my things.

He said, "What's going on?"

"I just quit! Mr. N cannot treat or talk to me however he wants. I'll be back later to get the rest of my things." I snatched my dignity and walked out the door.

Mr. N followed me as far as the parking lot.

I got into my car, pissed from what just occurred, and tried to figure how my life was about to change. I worked there long enough to realize that the money wasn't worth it! I sold my soul and my values. On the long drive home, I swore that I would turn this mess into something for the better.

This incident occurred in September. By December, I opened my own company, Chef's Secrets. I planned to expand it to include a unique cooking school; however, at that time of year, work for a culinarian was plentiful! I fell into the world of catering and have not launched the school...yet.

God was on my side. Every time I needed work, my phone rang. The offers did not set me up for financial independence, but they were enough to keep me going and reaffirm that I had done the right thing.

A good friend, Chef Eddie Wilson, worked for a catering company that specialized in executing large, high-profile events all over the country. They were in need of competent employees and top-quality chefs. He called to see if I knew anyone who could help him with an event at a horse park in Lexington, Kentucky.

"Of course!"

Lobster Enchilada with Jalapeño Marmalade

Serves 4

This dish was a signature item at the club. Although already established when I arrived, I perfected it. Visiting guests asked me to send this recipe to their club chefs, hopeful that it would be added to their menus. This dish is lots of work, but it is well worth the effort.

Lobster Sauce
2 tablespoons olive oil
1 cup shallots, minced
1 cup brandy
1 cup tequila
1 quart lobster stock
¼ cup tomato paste
1 teaspoon cayenne pepper
1 teaspoon ancho chili powder
4 tablespoons paprika
4 tablespoons dark chili powder
3 tablespoons cumin
½ cup butter
½ cup flour
Salt and pepper to taste

Pre-heat oil in saucepan. Add shallots and caramelize. Add liquor. Flame off alcohol and reduce by half. Add lobster stock and reduce by half. Add tomato paste and seasonings, then bring to a boil.

To form a roux, mix equal parts of melted butter and flour. Combine into a thick paste.

Add roux to lobster sauce to thicken. Reduce to low heat and simmer for 1 hour. Adjust seasoning to taste. Strain lobster sauce through a fine sieve/strainer. Set aside.

Jalapeño Marmalade
2 tablespoons olive oil
¼ cup shallots, minced
2 cloves garlic, minced
2 cups port wine
2 cups currant jelly
½ cup diced green chilies
1 large jalapeño, small diced
½ teaspoon ancho chili powder
1 tablespoon dark chili powder
1 tablespoon paprika
2 teaspoons cumin
¼ cup cornstarch, mixed with water for thickening

Pre-heat oil in saucepan. Add shallots, garlic and caramelize. Add seasonings and cook for 2 minutes. Add wine and reduce by half. Add jelly, chilies, jalapeño, chili powders, paprika, and cumin. Cook for 1 hour. Thicken with cornstarch mixture and cook for 10 more minutes. Set aside.

Lobster Enchiladas
2 1¼-pound fresh lobsters, cooked and all meat removed and small diced
4 6-inch flour tortillas, charred on one side
Red and green bell peppers, julienne

Cilantro leaves

Heat lobster sauce and meat. Place mixture on charred tortilla. Fold both sides to a V-shape, leaving meat and sauce exposed. Place warm marmalade on one side of the V and lobster sauce on the other. Garnish with julienned red and green bell peppers and fresh cilantro leaves. Serve immediately.

Traveling the Midwest

And just like that, I was in Kentucky for the Rolex Equestrian Time Trials. Is God good or what? Some of the most expensive horses in the world were showcased. These valuable stallions required a full-time contingent of Kentucky State Troopers to secure the investments.

Catering is quite different from restaurants and private clubs. Many aspects, beyond food, affect the success or failure of a catered event. I learned on the job, getting beat up for my inexperience. I was lucky to have teamed with a good crew because, believe me, it could've been much worse.

Two guys were professional caterers: the friend who got me started and one of his good friends. This remarkable duo were excellent chefs who excelled at practically everything else. Setup was child's play to them. Mastery of attire, equipment, and execution was shadowed by their knowledge.

They knew how to operate vehicles like forklifts, trucks, and tractors. They knew how to create a compound: pitch tents, set up cooking equipment and design a safe, efficient traffic flow.

I watched these guys in amazement as they breezed through like it was nothing. Since my only responsibility was the food, sometimes they looked at me, laughed, and shook their heads. It didn't matter if I was in a converted parking lot, cornfield, or racetrack, I did food better than they ever had.

Most caterers take shortcuts to get food out, especially on site. Delivered food is about 80% complete. Caterers are expected to add garnish, finishing touches, and TLC to enhance the presentation to guests. Whether due to time or budget constraints, lazy caterers slack on execution. Appalling to those of us who commit to excellence.

No matter how proficient I became with the other aspects of executing a pleasant off-site catering experience, my expertise is always food. As a result, I only did events with people with strengths in my blind spots. I had several memorable experiences in catering, which made me a better chef and leader.

For the Kentucky event, I was grouped with five staff members who traveled to and from the compound together. The first of twelve days was a sun-up-to-sun-down butt whipping for the entire staff. To lessen the end-of-the-day stress, management offered us beers. Since, I have never had a drink or taken drugs, I declined. My co-workers, however, enjoyed multiple brews.

An hour later, when folks were tipsy to 100% intoxicated, it was time to go to the hotel. Everyone scrambled for rides. The designated driver for my group was unfit to drive, so he tossed the keys to another drunkard. As we walked to the car, we picked up extra riders, but I was not letting any of them drive.

"Give me those freaking keys!"

By the time we reached the car, we were a party of fifteen. My seat was safe; however, the group was too big for the white Ford LTD station wagon. With simulated wood panels along the sides, this old school boat was typically driven by grandparents. I would never be caught dead in a car like this in Detroit, let alone drive it. We trimmed down to eleven riders.

They don't care how they get to the hotel. "Pack 'em in! Let's roll."

Some passengers wanted to smoke, and some were hot. So we rolled down the windows. Smoke billowed out as heads, legs, and arms bopped all over the place. After five minutes of this crap, I sped and weaved over the road, hurrying to get my butt out of the car.

Someone from the back of the car said, "I'm hungry."

How do you work around food all day and leave hungry? A Waffle House was across the street from the hotel, but I decided drive-thru was a better option. I pulled up to the speaker at a burger chain and tried to place orders for everyone. Beyond having a hard time hearing simultaneous food requests, my passengers couldn't read the menu, changed orders, and yelled out how much money they needed.

"Listen, you guys are destroying my reputation! My name is gonna be mud, and I'll get no love in Kentucky."

The young lady on the receiving end of the speaker erupted into boisterous laughter. When we pulled around, she looked at the circus-clown packed car and then ran to the other window for a better look. She and the cashier fell over laughing. They corralled the other workers to watch the comedy sketch. We shut down the restaurant for about three minutes as they had a good laugh at our expense. The cashier apparently felt sorry for me because she didn't charge me for my food. As embarrassed as I was, I don't think my passengers had a clue. But I'm sure the burger-joint employees talked about us for a long time.

Another Midwest incident that brings a smile to my face was when I worked with Chef Eddie, the caterer extraordinaire, and a different cast of characters on an auto racing series. Management wanted a consistent core group of leaders; however, the turnover rate in catering is high, so you work with new people all the time. Our assignment was simple: arrive at a track (in the middle of nowhere) midweek, then build a compound which included a kitchen and dining area. Everything needed to be ready Wednesday evening for food service Thursday through Sunday. For this series, we fed drivers, pit crew, media, and guests. We served breakfast, lunch, and dinner to 100-300 people, with breakfast least attended. The first day was most challenging as staff had a learning curve.

The company owner, Mrs. V, was a penny pincher. She cut us to the wire, never giving enough time to set up or resources to do the job properly. As we hurried through setup, Chef Eddie and I got the kitchen and compound together. As soon as we finished one thing, we pivoted to the next. We performed at maximum effort the entire event. The clock ticked, and the owner pushed for more. Although we had to work at top speed, we became good at it. We had systems down to a science and, like the race cars, ran like a fine-tuned machine.

We had inclement weather for four consecutive days: rain, cold, and high winds. At the end of the weekend, when it was time to go home, God let the sun shine. However, the rain had soaked most of our stuff. Everything had to be washed and dried, which was a time-consuming, pain-in-the-you-know-what task. The effort to salvage some items was ridiculous, especially the outdoor carpet which was a few feet shy of a football field.

In the middle of a cornfield, we had a carpeted tent for all our guests. Not only did it provide aesthetic qualities, but it also minimized the flying dirt and dust, which morphed to mud in the typhoon. As we broke down the compound, I assumed the mud-tracked carpet would be thrown away, but no. The owner wanted to keep it, so we had to clean and pack it for the ride.

The dining staff rinsed and dried it as best they could by placing it across a fence. Short on time, we had to pack it damp. We rolled up the extremely heavy rug and had to haul it to the top of the 10-foot trailer.

Since my area was broken down, I was assigned to help. Several guys and I tried to walk the rug up a ladder. We messed with that remnant for over thirty minutes. In the process, debris and mud splashed us into mental and physical exhaustion. After a few frustrating and animated attempts, F-bombs dropped.

I said, "Stop! Let me get more help." I called over Chef Eddie.

He stepped back to assess the situation, made some calculations, and figured out a plan. He laughed without restraint. "You guys will never be able to get that carpet on the trailer that way." He snorted. "Whose idea was this anyway?"

No one admitted to leading the fiasco.

Two minutes into his laughing, he said, "Get me some rope." He explained what needed to happen. He tied a knot and wrapped the rope around one end of the carpet. He slung the rest of the rope over the top of the trailer. After this, he told us to separate. Some went over to the rope end and a couple of us went on top.

"Some of you grab the rope on this end. Two get on top, and the rest on the other end. You guys on the bottom pull and hoist the carpet up to the guys on top." He looked up at me and the other guy standing on the trailer. "Once you get the carpet, secure it for the ride."

With a few effortless tugs, the carpet was locked and loaded.

I said, "Hey, man. Where did you learn how to do that?"

"Keith, you know I used to be a marine. Before that, I was a boy scout. As a scout leader growing up in Colorado, we always hiked and did all kinds of outdoor activities. That right there," he pointed to the anchored carpet, "is nothing."

In the city, we didn't have many outdoor experiences unless you count running from the cops or any other pursuer. I knew which allies to run through and fences to jump. Great street skills, but not transferable for culinary.

Lesson learned: how you respond to situations determines your enjoyment or lack thereof. My best advice is to surround yourself with people from whom you can learn; you will always have a positive learning experience.

Roasted Asparagus with Balsamic Syrup

Serves 4

At this point in my career, I catered all over the country. My meals consisted of fast, fried foods. Realizing that I needed to take better care of myself, I incorporated more vegetables and salads into my diet. This easy recipe is delicious. I enjoy it with a baked potato or rice and don't need a protein to be full.

1 pound medium asparagus spears, trim off woody bottom about ¼ inch up spear
3 tablespoons olive oil
Kosher salt and fresh ground black pepper to taste
2 cups balsamic vinegar
½ cup honey
Juice of 1 fresh lemon

Preheat oven to 425°F. Place asparagus on roasting pan, making sure it lies flat. Drizzle with olive oil. Season with salt and pepper. Roast in oven for 10-12 minutes. Remove from oven and let cool to room temperature.

Place vinegar, lemon juice, and honey in a pot. Bring to a boil and reduce to simmer. Cook until mixture reaches syrup consistency. Cool slightly and pour syrup into a squirt bottle. Place asparagus on a serving platter and drizzle with syrup.

Salt Lake City, Olympic Village

I stayed with my formula of catering and other culinary jobs for several years. One of the largest events I did was the 2002 Winter Olympics in Salt Lake City.

A catering company from New York joined forces with a local caterer to create a new company. They booked a significant amount of the available business, serving everything from boxed lunches to high-dollar gourmet meals. They needed service staff, executive chefs, and everything in between.

A good friend, Chef Dave, contacted me to see if I was interested.

Right time, right place, and a perfect fit for my business model. "Absolutely."

Of course, the process wasn't that easy. My initial interview was eight months prior to the event followed by a series of security background checks. Portions of the contract started more than a year in advance, but I came on board for about six weeks, mid-January through February. Thousands were hired to execute contracts.

To my favor, I was in charge of the official USA communication compound. Every athlete who won a medal came to our venue to get their security credentials for the awards ceremony. AT&T and a host of other sponsors turned a nightclub into the official headquarters. They hired the club staff, including the owner and bartenders, to be on call to do whatever was needed for the guests.

Satellites, computers, TVs, and phones were installed to make it a first-class communications hub. All the athletes, their families, and friends were encouraged to take care of any of their communication needs: emails, phone calls, or whatever, to whomever anywhere in the world. If Aunt Sally couldn't attend in person, she was welcomed to participate virtually from our venue. Inclement weather? Mom can't get up the mountain to watch her loved one compete? No problem. She could watch the segment broadcasted in our heated, comfortable, two-level venue. Operations ran from 7 AM to 10 PM. We served breakfast, lunch, and dinner from double-sided buffets.

Management planned to have a main kitchen commissary to produce most of the food, then shuttle it to satellite kitchens for on-site staff to finish it for service. My responsibility was to oversee the build out of the delivered food to execute in excellence. A simple plan that was complicated when the head chef quit in November. His unplanned departure left the company scrambling to fulfill the contractual agreement. By the time they replaced him, it was far too late.

When I arrived several weeks later, I witnessed the domino effect of repercussions. The new chef sat in the commissary office crying. The health department tried to pinpoint who gave instructions to chill soups, sauces, etc. with a new innovation.

They ran out of the ice wands, big plastic sticks filled with frozen water to cool hot food in a quick, safe, and sanitary manner. Some genius suggested placing ice in garbage bags to create the same effect...not! The ice melted, the product wasn't properly chilled, and garbage bags of lukewarm water set in the food containers.

The inspector was livid. He demanded that all suspect product be destroyed. Since the chef was out of commission, an assistant chef and a couple of managers were chastised.

The inspector barked action, but they weren't moving fast enough. A significant amount of product scheduled to be served soon was in question, so the staff tried to salvage it.

The inspector abruptly left and returned with two containers. He doused the suspect product with bleach. "Get rid of this product now!"

Culinarians and health inspectors have an adversarial relationship at best. Add the fact that we were serving our country's top athletes and you can imagine the level of stress and tension.

Management blasted the staff, holding them responsible for the incident. Although no one confessed, someone gave unauthorized approval to poison people.

When I watched the fiasco unfold, I wanted to meet with the chef to assess the operation. He was overwhelmed as this event was far beyond his pay grade and expertise. My immediate thought was, *No, thank you. I'll pass.* I didn't want anything to do with that debacle. I'd much rather slip into obscurity and get out of there. Instead, I assisted with prep for a few hours since my venue didn't start for a couple of days.

Glad that I wasn't assigned to work in the commissary, an escort took me to my new home: an apartment complex just outside the city. I stayed in a three-bedroom unit with eight other guys.

One person worked in the kitchen with me. The rest were service staff or bartenders. One guy was from Jamaica and another from South Korea. The Jamaican asked us to pool our monies to buy soap, toilet paper, paper towels, and food. Everyone agreed except the South Korean. He put in less money because he didn't contribute toward food. He told us that he was a starving college student and needed to walk away with as much of his money as possible. He had three cases of ramen noodles and a hot plate next to his bed, his diet for the entire stay. I didn't need to contribute toward food, but I did to help the rest of the guys. If I work a food job and am hungry during the experience, shame on me.

Working different venues and shifts, people came and went all day. A shuttle service was available while some folks took public transportation. A couple of guys on the service staff for the Nike tent got fresh gear every shift. I was so jealous.

I visited my venue, the converted nightclub, a couple of days early. After meeting the staff, I cleaned the place. The kitchen didn't have much to offer other than refrigeration and limited cooking equipment. An outside contractor was hired to run the club's food program. He obviously took advantage and ran the place into the ground. A pigsty.

The contractor prepared bar food: fried items, burgers, sandwiches, and appetizers, which left lots to be desired. The food program negatively affected the owner's sales.

When Mr. S, the club owner, saw me cleaning the place, he was ecstatic. I introduced myself followed by a great conversation about career, family, and food. The competency and quality of the staff was a major concern of the caterer and client. Each wanted a committed, dedicated professional to run their operation.

Mr. S contacted the caterer to inform him that I was his guy. "Don't even think about moving him or sending me any other supervisors." Since his spot was home to one of the largest clients, high-profile and spending a ton of money, he had a voice and used it.

I got his kitchen and equipment cleaned and spent time with his service staff. I developed a team atmosphere, which would pay long-term dividends.

We had a month of menus for each service and received daily deliveries from the commissary. The goal was receipt of food that's about 80% ready and finish it on site. The first delivery was wrong. It took me about ten minutes to make changes and inform management on both ends.

When I told Mr. S, he smiled wide. "Go ahead and do your thing, Keith. I'm just happy you're here. I know I'm in good hands."

His words made me feel so good. "As long as you see me, you don't have anything to worry about on the food side. I'll make sure everything is under control." I had issues with the commissary throughout the run but handled each one without disrupting food service. I barked a bit in the beginning. But, once the commissary staff understood my expectations, they delivered my items early and in good shape. One hiccup, not caused by food indigestion, was rather large.

Several of my support staff griped after they didn't receive their paychecks. Openly frustrated, they discussed not showing up for work. When I got wind of the pending mutiny, I addressed it. I knew that I could not execute this mammoth event with less staff. I didn't get my money either, but I didn't lash out like my crew.

Once Mr. S found out, he said, "Keith, let me know if you need my help to fix this. All I have to do is make a call and things will happen right away, if you know what I mean?" He flashed a wry smile. He had people who were built for retrieving monies owed.

Everyone got paid about a week late and wanted to run to the bank to make sure the funds were there.

We closed the run with two parties: one for the client, AT&T, and the other for staff. The client was so happy that they gave gifts and bonuses to the team. The main contact let me know how pleased he was with my performance. He explained that, six months prior, he worried about how everything would come together. As the event got closer, the pressure intensified. Once he was comfortable with the venue, his anxiety shifted to the food and staff. Having put me through his rigorous interview process, he knew I was a keeper.

"The very first thing I did every day was check on you. When I saw you in the kitchen, I knew that I didn't have anything to worry about with the food."

What a compliment from such a high-ranking official, conducting this world-class event.

The staff party was similar. Mr. S and his team gave me a standing ovation. They thanked me for exceeding their expectations. Several staff members told me that they were proud of the food we served.

Mr. S offered me the food service contract for the club. "I'll do whatever's necessary to get you to take it over."

I was touched and flattered, but the timing wasn't right. I declined his gracious offer.

Dare I say, "Well done!"

Coming down from the high of this event was brutal. I did not understand why things weren't happening as fast as I hoped. I thought I did everything necessary to skyrocket my professional status, but I was stuck in neutral. God kept my phone ringing almost every time I needed money, which was confirmation that I was on the right path.

Somewhat protected in my own small culinary world, I lacked experience; however, I got plenty accepting many large catering jobs.

One fascinating thing about the culinary profession is that you meet people from all over the world. Most of whom are actively pursuing their dreams. I love these encounters because it forces me to re-evaluate my situation.

I feed off their determination and said to myself, "Come on, Keith. Get your act together and make yours happen. If they can do it, you can, too!"

At times, I lose focus, especially on long-term goals, get easily distracted, and become consumed with the task at hand.

> "Don't be afraid to fail big to dream big. But remember, dreams without goals are just dreams, which ultimately fuel disappointment. I try to give myself a goal every day."
> —Denzel Washington

Whatever your goals, stay focused and organized. Work on them. Even a little day-by-day will move you closer to fulfilling them. It took me a long time to learn this lesson. After I elevated myself, I met another angel who helped me further shape my dream. Recall the interview with a local magazine I mentioned on page 38. During the conversation, I stated that I wanted to do TV and ultimately have my own show. I put it into the atmosphere, and God listened.

Busy doing my normal work, the phone rang.

"Hi, Chef Jones, you don't know me, but I'm also from Detroit. My wife gave me a magazine article featuring you. I just left a lucrative career to pursue my dream of making movies and TV shows. I'd like to help you make your dream come true!"

Best Meatloaf

Serves 6

As the head chef at the AT&T Compound for the Winter Olympics in Salt Lake City 2002, I took great pride in serving our athletes. Everyone enjoyed the meals; however, the most popular dishes were this meatloaf recipe and roasted chicken.

Meatloaf
½ cup celery, chopped fine
⅓ cup green onions, chopped fine
¼ cup green bell peppers, chopped fine
2 teaspoons garlic, chopped fine
2 tablespoons butter
1 pound ground beef
½ pound ground veal
½ pound ground pork or turkey
½ cup breadcrumbs
¼ cup fresh parsley, chopped fine
2 large eggs
2 teaspoons Worcestershire sauce
1½ teaspoons salt
½ teaspoon black pepper
½-1 cup ketchup (optional)

Preheat oven to 350°F. In a heavy skillet, cook celery, onions, peppers and garlic in butter for about 5 minutes. Combine all ingredients in a large mixing bowl. Using your hands, mix all remaining items until well-blended. Be careful not to over mix as this can cause your meatloaf to be too dense.

Shape mixture into a loaf and bake for 1½ hours or until it reaches an internal temperature of 170°F. If you choose, top the loaf with ketchup the last 20 minutes of baking. Remove from pan and serve immediately.

Gravy for Meatloaf
2 tablespoons drippings from meatloaf
2 tablespoons flour
1½ cups beef stock
Salt, pepper, and herbs to taste
Optional herbs to taste: thyme, parsley, and/or rosemary

Heat drippings to a boil in small pot. Slowly whisk in flour, making sure you blend until it's smooth. Cook this mixture until it develops a little color (looking for a light caramel color). Slowly add stock and whisk constantly as gravy thickens. Reduce heat and season with salt, pepper, and herbs.

Japan: I Hope I'm Worthy

The next day, I had an in-person meeting with Mr. Thomas. Nine months later, we were filming a show in Japan. Wow! God is good! The fantastic process changed my life, and I've walked to the beat of a different drummer ever since.

On a cold November day, we left Denver for a 16-hour flight: Denver to San Francisco to Tokyo. This international trip was a first for me. I experienced emotions from excited to scared-to-death.

Traveling to another country, meeting new people and cultures, trying different food, and filming my first TV show stimulated my excitement. The fear came from the reality of satisfying an investor, Mr. M, who invested his hard-earned money. I just wanted to break into the business without concern for fiscal obligation. I thought someone else was responsible for the business end. But when it's your dream, you must be all in for whatever it takes.

I had a 700-pound gorilla on my back; the investor who wanted his investment plus a profit. I often told myself, "You already know stress and pressure, so bring it. Let's do this."

Once we landed in Tokyo, we took a train to Yokohama. Public transportation is incredible over there.

Mr. M hired a local team to translate, navigate the city, and film. The camera crew was waiting for us at the Yokohama station.

A lean outfit, the two guys, from the United States and Europe, decided to make a living in Japan's film industry.

The owner, Dan Smith, was from the States. He met Mr. Thomas a couple of years earlier at an international TV conference in Las Vegas. As retired military, he had done production work and entertainment activities for the bases where he was once stationed. He excelled in editing; however, his primary responsibility was in front of the camera as the host of his own TV show. His assistant, Ricardo Columbo, was an accomplished photographer who spoke fluent Japanese. They were as hungry for this opportunity as we were.

We put our luggage in the car and drove to a local restaurant to get to know each other. We decided to get as much footage as possible based on the schedule the boss, Mr. M, had set.

Dan looked at me. "I know you want to do TV, and I want to make you the best show possible! My motive is simple: I want to have content on TV in the US market. Your show will be my first opportunity to do that. It's a done deal here. I'll put your content in this market in five-minute bumpers, which we'll drop into our existing shows. Your team will string those segments together and finish the show for distribution in the States. Are you ready for this?"

"Absolutely! I'm ready for the challenge. I've been waiting for this for a long time. You have no idea."

"Okay. I hear you. I just want you to understand that we're taking a chance on each another to make this shot work. Failure is not an option. I'm going to push you to get what I need, no exception."

"Awesome. I wouldn't have it any other way."

Once we got the business out of the way, we enjoyed dinner. We traveled halfway across the world to eat pizza in Japan. Although different from "American" pizza with its olive-oil base, thin-sliced potatoes, and minimal cheese, we enjoyed the meal.

They drove us to our temporary home, a boarding house not too far from the restaurant. The three-level house had 30-40 sleeping rooms, a community kitchen, family room, and gender-specific bathrooms. We each had a room with a window, closet, thermostat, and light. I made a pallet on the floor with the pad, pillow, and blankets provided. Basic accommodations sufficient for the mission: film the show and protect the executive producer's investment.

The local crew emphasized the need to adjust to the fifteen-hour time difference. They suggested that we avoid sleeping. I laid on that floor and crashed.

The next day, we caught a two-hour flight to the island of Okinawa. We were scheduled to film for five days, focusing on the Air Force and local tourist spots. I found it comical that we were the only Americans on the plane. The safety instructions were explained in Japanese. I followed along, not because I understood the language, but because I was a seasoned flyer.

After the pre-flight tasks, I leaned over and said to one of the guys. "Hey, this is different having Japanese flight attendants."

"Most of these ladies aren't Japanese. They're Korean!"

How in the world do you know that?

The weather in Okinawa was incredible: sunshine, blue skies, and temperatures of 80-85°. A dramatic difference from the cold temps of the mainland. We dropped off our stuff at the hotel and went to Kadena Air Force Base.

Dan, the retired military boss, checked us in and introduced us to our base escorts. We scouted locations for interviews, film activities, and a store demo on the massive compound. We met a few people, shook hands, and grabbed a quick bite to eat. Before I knew it, we had to hustle back to the hotel. Mr. Thomas and I needed sleep, but the adrenaline rush was so great that we cruised on autopilot.

The store demo was standard. Tables displayed various products available for purchase. I used the ingredients to create recipes. The staff passed out samples until they were gone. A nice crowd of 100-150 gathered before I started the demo. Instead of young adult to middle-aged women, my typical crowd, this group was mainly men, some in uniform and others with their families.

I said, "Thank you for coming. I'm Chef Keith Denard Jones. I just arrived from Denver, Colorado, and I'm thrilled to be here. When I left, it was snowing. So your beautiful weather makes me extremely happy."

A young soldier said, "Excuse me, I'm from Denver. Can you tell me where in Denver you live?"

"Aurora."

"Hey, I know Aurora. I have relatives there. Where in Aurora?"

"Well okay, then. I'm near Quincy and Parker Roads."

"Is that by the Cherry Creek Reservoir?"

"Exactly!"

We smiled and laughed. Our brief exchange super-energized me. I rocked the house, putting on one of my better, if not the best, performances. Everyone laughed, conversed, and had a good time.

When I finished, a few people came to talk to me. Before I knew it, my groupie line was 75-people deep. They wanted my autograph. Are you kidding me? The only signatures I gave were to guarantee loans or approve food orders. On the inside, I was overwhelmed; on the outside, I was cool. Since nothing like this had ever happened to me, I was determined to accommodate every person. Schedule? What schedule? Stop the program! Let's capture and enjoy this moment.

At the end of the line, stood the soldier with whom I had spoken earlier. He said, "Thank you so much for coming over here. I didn't know we meant that much to you folks at home. I have something for you." He extended his hand. As we shook hands, he gently placed something in my hand.

"No, no, no. Your money is no good! Please, I don't need it"

"It's not money." He smiled and then walked away.

I put his gift in my pocket and finished visiting with the guests.

As the team broke down the equipment, a base escort said, "We went over our time limit and missed the next event. Can I take you to the Officers' Club for food and drinks?"

"Absolutely. That sounds like a great idea."

Once inside, we sat, relaxed, and ordered. As we waited for our food, we recapped the demo.

"Can you believe what just happened?"

Mr. Thomas said, "Keith, you just became a star! These folks had no idea who you were. But after today, they'll never forget you."

Ecstatic and amazed, I did my best to stay humble and grateful. If the rest of the month-long trip was like today, my anticipation soared.

We were enjoying the meal when I remembered the soldier's gift. I reached in my pocket and pulled it out. "Hey, Mr. Thomas. Look at what I got." The matted bronze coin had images and inscriptions on both sides. Thicker and bigger than a silver dollar, it weighed about a pound. I handed it to him.

He flipped the coin through his fingers. "I have no idea what it is. Where did you get it?"

"You remember the soldier from Denver? He gave it to me." I turned to our escort. "Can you tell us what this is?"

"Let me see that." Shocked, he spoke in an excited tone. "Where did you get this?"

"A soldier at the demo gave it to me."

He called over a couple of officers. "Look at what the chef got!"

They asked, "Where did he get it?"

The escort said, "Chef said that a soldier at his demo gave it to him."

I'm freaking out. *What in the world is this thing?* "Can somebody please tell me what it is?"

The escort gathered the team. "What you have is a medal. It's given to soldiers for doing something above and beyond the call of duty. It takes on average two-and-one-half years to get one. I cannot believe you got this on your first day!"

I'm not worthy. I cried. I looked at Mr. Thomas. "I've got to find that young man and give this medal back to him. There's no way I can keep this."

"Absolutely not. You don't know where that young man is in his life, but you touched him to the point where he felt compelled to give it to you. Accept it. Keep it and honor him. That's all you should do."

I cried, thinking about the soldiers and the sacrifices they make. They put their lives—and those of their families—on the line making sure I have the freedom to do what I want, go where I want, and think and believe what I want. And he gave *me* a medal? I honor him with every performance and demonstration! His gracious gift changed me forever. I pray that we'll meet again. And, when we do,

I hope that I am still worthy of the honor he bestowed on me.

Dare I say, "Well done!"

We had incredible experiences with many other soldiers and officers, notably Sergeants Rambo and MacGyver. We shadowed them for a day, learning their responsibilities and the equipment they used. These soldiers were at the highest of their craft. They dealt with life-and-death issues, yet they took time to smile, laugh, and joke with me.

On another occasion, I spoke with a young female officer who was in charge of a refueling plane.

I asked, "How did you know you wanted to fly a plane?"

"I had no idea when I joined, but after understanding what it required, I decided to go for it. And here I am."

Because the production manager had firsthand knowledge of military life, we had one-of-a-kind, behind-the-scenes access to capture quality footage. We met military firefighters who geared up for Thanksgiving turkey frying by ensuring it was safe. A soldier, who cooked in one of the Officer's Clubs, took pride in everything she did. Even boxed lunches had to be composed in a specific way. We filmed segments with a variety of servicemen and women. So many dedicated people, so many moments, so many memories.

A buzz swelled throughout the base about "this chef guy." Requests to meet me and be on the show came in at a steady rate. We did our best to accommodate them all. We worked crazy hours. And when we weren't filming, the production guys were editing.

We previewed a rough draft of the edited footage with the base commander. Already aware of our visit to the base, he looked at me. "Who are you?"

"Excuse me?"

"Who are you?"

Confused, I looked at Mr. Thomas for assistance on how to answer him.

The commander said, "I've been at this base for seven years. All kinds of entertainers have come and gone, but never has anyone created this much excitement!" He watched the segment with the sergeants. "I mean look at this footage. These guys are serious about what they do, and they're the best of the best. You'd never know they make critical life-and-death decisions the way they're smiling and laughing it up with you. I have never seen them act like this."

I bubbled on the inside but said nothing. I looked at my team and then locked eyes with Mr. Thomas.

He said, "He's just a chef from Colorado over here to do a TV show."

The base commander said, "He's much more than that, so much more. He's special. I never had anyone have this kind of effect on my base. Do you mind if we spread the word?"

Dan said, "No, not at all. Go right ahead."

An endorsement from the top dog? What a tremendous vote of confidence. We were promoted as something positive for the soldiers and overall morale. The requests escalated. Because our itinerary was already packed full, we waited to see if any of the scheduled activities were canceled to fill the demand. The likelihood of cancellation was low because we had a good mix of off-base events with retired military personnel. These folks owned businesses and oozed talent. They chased their dreams in Okinawa without thinking about returning to the States.

We returned to the mainland re-energized and ready to go! With us better understanding one another, we developed an organic chemistry, working together instinctively.

What was interesting about working in the local communities was that the people had no idea I was a chef. I didn't wear the traditional chef's uniform: white jacket and hounds-tooth pants. I wore tailored uniforms with cuff, collar, and front cording accents. I had four different jacket styles in various colors with logos and matching button combinations. Many mainlanders assumed I was an entertainer. When they realized my mastery was food, they covered their faces and blushed.

Almost every person we encountered had an endearing quality: respectful. We visited restaurants from hole-in-the-wall noodle shops to one of the most expensive places in the world, the Tokyo American Club.

A memorable stop was in Takayama, a sister city to Denver. We had a couple of shoots planned and needed flexibility the train could not accommodate, so we rented a car for the almost six-hour drive. The team members loaded the car with the gear the night before for a 3 AM departure.

I tried hard to stay awake, but I slept through the night portion of the drive. When daylight broke, I awoke to a jungle. We went through a series of tunnels and bridges. We saw all types of wildlife indigenous to mountainous areas.

Mr. Thomas was in and out of consciousness the duration of the trip. On one of his woke bouts, he looked out the window. He sat up in his seat and pointed. "Hey! What is that on the side of the road? Look out for those kids! What are their parents thinking letting them play so close to the road?"

As we got closer, we were amazed—and relieved—to find that the kids were baboons. Prior to this excursion, I had only seen baboons captive in a zoo. We had to stop, watch, and capture the sight on film.

Dan, the production manager, said, "Sorry, guys. We have a schedule to keep. Slowing down to watch the little time we did put us behind." He was great at keeping us on point.

No footage, only memories.

Takayama was a beautiful, scenic mountain town known for its sake (fermented rice) breweries. They had six facilities within one block. The strategy was to show evidence of our visit to Denver officials. Dan secured an interview with Takayama's mayor. Excited to meet him, I extended my hand for a handshake, but Mr. Thomas caught me in time. Touching is deemed disrespectful, especially at the mayor's level. The Japanese culture is about bowing.

The mayor spoke with us about twenty minutes through translators. We received a warm welcome to his city as he treated us like foreign dignitaries. He assigned two of his staff members to escort us for lunch and a city tour.

They took us to Suzuya Restaurant, a highly-recognized restaurant, and spared no expense. The restaurant featured local pickled vegetables in a food fest that kept coming. We cooked some at the table, hot-pot style. Flavored broth simmered at the table. Raw ingredients were placed into the hot pot and cooked to desired doneness. Similar to fondue, the cooked food is often paired with dipping sauces and garnishes. The amazing video footage took almost three hours to capture.

As we broke down, a chef asked to make us his signature dish. He didn't wait for an answer but whipped together a scrambled egg dish flavored with pickled vegetables. He served it on individual sizzle platters with vegetables in the middle, surrounded by eggs and garnished with julienned nori (dry seaweed with a savory, salty taste).

I looked at Mr. Thomas. "I can't eat another bite. I don't like scrambled eggs, and I'm good on the pickled vegetables. You guys go ahead and dig in."

Under the radar to spare me embarrassment, he said, "You've got to be kidding me. They're doing this for you...the chef. You better suck it up and eat some. Are you trying to disrespect these folks? You trying to create an international incident?"

He was right. As a chef, people offer me food for an expert opinion. After a quick attitude adjustment, I ate most of it. The dish was oishī, which is Japanese for delicious.

The night concluded with what seemed like a ceremony. The restaurant staff formed a line, bowed as we passed, and thanked us for visiting.

The hosts took us to the sake breweries and tourist attractions. We stayed about two hours longer than planned, which Dan said that he'd make up on the drive home.

Most of the schedule required public transportation because automobiles were too expensive to rent. The subway station was almost three miles away. The walk took about 45 minutes because we had so much equipment. Lugging all the gear from place to place had to be a comical sight. By the time we returned home, I had lost close to eighteen pounds.

Many fond memories fill me with warmth. Simple things like walking the streets of Chinatown where most of the people were several inches shorter than me, and the press conference promoting a movie.

When we weren't getting in his way, Dan was connected to all kinds of show-business activities. Before the conference, he gave us a five-minute etiquette lesson. At show time, the team swung into action.

I've seen lots of movie premiers on TV but never from the vantage point of behind-the-scenes. Cool. Mr. Thomas and I took our seats in the front area designated for reporters. We waited an hour for the A-list celebrity to arrive. Photographers lined up on a platform in the back of the room with their gear primed and ready. The room was quiet except for the two of us and faint whispers from the photographers.

Tom Hanks walked on stage with an entourage of interpreters, movie executives, and assistants to promote *Polar Express,* a family Christmas movie that debuted in 2004. The audience was polite. No one talked or moved in their seats during the presentation. When they opened the floor for questions, reporters raised their hands and waited for approval to speak.

Mr. Thomas tapped me on the back. "Go ahead and raise your hand."

"I can't do that. We're not even supposed to be in the room. We're only here because of Dan."

"You're just scared. I bet he'd be happy to hear someone speaking English. Go ahead and raise your hand. Only two things can happen: he'll call on you or he won't."

Nervous. Sweat poured from under my arms. My hands were cold and clammy.

"Raise your hand unless you're a *punk*. We did not come all the way here for you to punk out." He cackled like a chicken.

I thrust up my hand strong, tall, and proud. After he acknowledged me, I said, "Hi, my name is Keith Jones. I'm a chef from the United States filming my TV show. What do you like to eat here in Japan?"

He chuckled. "Thank you very much for your question."

I think I caught him off guard because I didn't ask about the movie.

"I enjoy noodles." He paused. "How about you join me on stage for a skit?"

A signature line of the movie was said by the train conductor, played by Tom Hanks. He had us practice a couple times and then in unison, we yelled, "All aboard!"

After the three-minute exchange, I floated on cloud nine back to my seat. I will remember him and that moment for the rest of my life.

Mr. Thomas tapped my shoulder. "You did it! You're the man. I'm so proud of you. The only way that goes down is with the help of God! We're blessed and on the right path."

The rest of the month flew by in a blur. We filmed five or six segments a day. When we got on the plane headed to the States, Mr. Thomas and I talked about the visit from wheels up to wheels down, minus eating and restroom breaks. We devised a plan to capitalize on the Japan experience.

We arrived at LAX and headed to customs. I wanted to rush to the front of the line; however, my travel companion wasn't in a hurry. I followed his lead and stayed next to him.

When he showed the agent his passport, the agent said, "Where are you coming from?"

"Me and the gentleman behind me are coming from Japan."

"I just watched a show about Black people doing their thing in Japan on Colours TV Network. Dan Smith, a cool dude, hosted *Black Life in Japan*."

"Really? That's unbelievable. I'm an executive with that network. I spent the last month in Japan with Mr. Smith filming a TV show for the guy behind me."

His expression of surprise and amazement was priceless. He shook Mr. Thomas's hand. "You can go on through." He waved me through, too. No hassles, no questions, nothing.

Mr. Thomas and Dan didn't delay to complete editing to produce a full show to air in the States. Dan was highly recognized and accomplished in Japan. He had several shows airing in that market and movie segments in markets across the world. He included pre-produced segments featuring a who's who of the world's largest entertainment personalities. Celebrities including Will Smith, Tom Cruise, Jamie Foxx, Gwyneth Paltrow, and Beyoncé commented on food and life in Japan, giving our show credibility that no other food show had. My angel worked hard and got the show done. The fast-paced show was a combination of several elements—cooking, travel, entertainment, and interviews—which made it enjoyable to watch. I was proud of the finished product.

The next step was approval from the investor: judge, jury, and executioner. After waiting for what seemed like forever, he rated it. Thumbs down. He liked the show but had issues with the celebrity segments. Per his lawyer's advice, the investor instructed us to remove them.

We made the recommended changes, which left each episode with a gap up to eight-minutes long. With Dan's involvement, the show was already airing in Japan. For airtime in the US, we had to create new footage, which the investor funded.

We contacted the owner of a talent agency we met while in Japan. We explained the situation, then worked out a deal to bring in one of his guys. Because we could not replace segment for segment, we shifted from zero studio content to more than 70%. Earl, owner of a talent agency, selected a smooth jazz phenomenon who sat in the kitchen and played as I cooked. His musical contribution made our show unique. It took two full days to complete thirteen episodes. The new show was completely different from its Asian cousin. I liked it better because of the studio chemistry we developed. However, removing the celebrity content, the most appealing selling aspect of the show, caused it to die on the cutting room floor.

A few networks expressed interest in the original version. Once they discovered the celebrity segments were replaced, they changed position on the compensation offer. Instead of paying us for the show, they wanted to charge us to air it. The executive producer (EP), our investor businessman extraordinaire, opposed and took a hardline stance: no pay, no play.

Crushed. That show was a culmination of my blood, sweat, tears, and years of effort. I went from the highest of highs to the lowest of lows in two weeks. Since the EP didn't have any emotional attachment to the project, he made a sound financial decision. Intimidated by his ability to pull the financial plug at any minute, I couldn't muster the courage to influence him to change his mind.

Almost on cue, Mr. Thomas put it in perspective. Although it didn't look like I envisioned, I accomplished my goal of having a TV show. *Champagne Chef* got positive responses in the limited market and boosted my experience and confidence.

Because of Dan's busy schedule, he moved to his next assignment. We didn't reconnect to flush out residual opportunities.

I couldn't wallow in self-pity because I had to shrink my learning curve in the business side of television production. What elements make a show successful? How and where can I get funding or sponsorships? How do I produce it? How do I get it on TV? In multiple markets? How do I make a living doing it?

I had a life-defining moment: I can never go back into the kitchen. Not for lack of skill, but I did not want to deprive my other talents. People waited in line for my autograph. They wanted to talk to me, shake my hand, and touch me. How could I return to the kitchen without trying to figure out what I could ultimately achieve? I believed.

Working for someone else, I would have commanded top salary but sacrificed time to pursue my dreams. I needed flexibility. My dilemma was straightforward: how do I earn enough money to fulfill my obligations while moving forward with my vision?

Mr. Thomas committed to get the show on the air. He earned his living as an entrepreneur, so we were in the same boat. Over the years, we did many projects together including TV, movies, and music videos. Some gigs paid money, others paid experience. Always the student.

With experience and a solid reputation, I branded myself as the get-it-done-right chef, which allowed me to ease back into catering and cooking demonstrations. Some time ago, when I was chef at The Metropolitan Club, I befriended the daughter of a board member. She landed a job with an appliance distributor and called me to conduct demonstrations to help sell their products for home chefs. I also did cooking demonstrations for several professional cooking equipment manufacturers. I traveled to cities showing chefs, kitchen staff, managers, and owners how to operate equipment. The culmination of my side hustles paid the bills.

Working with the professional equipment manufacturers was perfect because they had a pool of chefs who were hired to conduct trainings and demonstrations. We had varying backgrounds and skill sets but were similar in one critical area: we owned our businesses. This feature gave the company flexibility to cover multiple assignments and allowed all of us to earn extra cash.

What started as win-win soon became an issue. In a good month, five assignments might result in fifteen days of work. As chefs realized the work wasn't consistent enough to maintain their lifestyle, they moved to other options. The remnant was a core group of four chefs who did most of the work.

One of the chefs used this strategy as his main source of income. He fought to get jobs, breaking the rules and doing whatever was necessary to stay booked. As the low person on the totem pole and living in a city with minimal sales, my job opportunities were few and far between. Having other income-producing opportunities on my plate, I didn't press for more.

One of the other chefs, Claudio Ferrer, also wanted his own TV show and then travel the country, making guest appearances, performing demonstrations, and inspiring people. I loved him like he was my brother and would do everything I could to help him achieve his goals.

> "You can have anything you want, if you help enough people get what they want."
> —Zig Ziglar

Blackened Buffalo Ribeye Steak with 5-Pepper Ale Demi-Glace

Serves 4

While filming *Champagne Chef* in Japan, we were exposed to great delicacies including pickled vegetables. Colorado is known for premium buffalo meat. This recipe is my gift back to Denver's sister city, Takayama, for sharing their best with us.

Blackening Spice Mixture
1 teaspoon chili powder
1 teaspoon ancho chili powder
1 teaspoon cumin powder
1 teaspoon garlic powder
1 teaspoon onion powder
½ teaspoon paprika
½ teaspoon oregano
½ teaspoon salt
½ teaspoon pepper
¼ teaspoon cayenne

Combine spices.

Buffalo Rib-Eye Steaks
4 each 12-16 oz. buffalo rib-eye steaks
1 oz. olive oil

Brush buffalo steaks with 1 oz. of the oil and season with spice mixture on both sides. Marinate in refrigerator for at least 6 hours.

Pre-heat oven to 400°F.

In a pre-heated cast iron skillet, blacken one side of steak until golden brown. Finish cooking in pre-heated oven until medium rare (3-5 minutes).

5-Pepper Ale Demi-Glace
1 shallot, minced
1 garlic clove, minced
1 oz. olive oil
1 cup micro-brewed beer
1 cup demi-glace
1 jalapeño pepper, deseeded and small diced
1 green pasilla pepper, deseeded and small diced
1 red bell pepper, deseeded and small diced
1 orange bell pepper, deseeded and small diced
1 yellow bell pepper, deseeded and small diced
1 tablespoon honey
1 tablespoon butter
Salt and pepper to taste

In a small saucepan, cook shallot and garlic in olive oil over medium heat until translucent. Stir occasionally for 5-7 minutes. Deglaze the pan with beer and reduce by half. Add glace and reduce to sauce consistency. Add peppers, honey, and butter. Season to taste and serve with buffalo steaks.

Ecuador: A Friend in Deed

Claudio Ferrer was originally from Argentina. He made his way to the United States as a young kid, overcame challenges, and elevated himself to one of the top chefs in the industry.

We first met at a chef's conference hosted by an equipment manufacturer. Twelve of us sat and listened to the corporate executive chef, with whom we had worked in the past. He was rebuilding his team and corralled us to cover the entire country and manage markets where the company hoped to sell equipment. In the casual setting, he stated his intention to form a super field team to support his distributor network.

As a chef, you learn the profession by working all kitchen positions. Then, educate yourself on the business side to round out your skills to become a competent executive chef. Once you "arrive," your responsibilities magnify. Cooking time dwindles as you focus on managing, or should I say, babysitting. After years of grinding, many chefs long to just cook and pursue different options like working for a professional equipment manufacturer.

Although the coveted corporate position was inviting, I was put in that room to meet Chef Claudio. We had much in common with the most endearing shared quality: big hearts. We helped almost anyone with a sincere cause. We gave tirelessly, without regard to our families, oftentimes putting ourselves out to help.

Based in Florida, he did events all over the world. He took me on a trip to Ecuador for the International Food Show.

Many neighboring countries participated, which brought big crowds. The event showcased new food items, new equipment, and culinary talent highlighted in a three-day cooking competition. Competitors were designated as student or professional. Talent from ten to twelve countries came from as far as Brazil. The community and culinary school, which sponsored our visit, supported the show. They brought in about thirty other people to help with the show.

They provided lodging in a hotel, which was also home for most of the competing teams. Oro Verde Guayaquil was a nice, four-star hotel. Guards holding automatic weapons were stationed at the front entry. Chef Claudio did not seem to be phased by the armed infantry, but I freaked out every time I saw them. *Am I safe here?*

Chef Claudio attended as a judge and chef presenter for the equipment manufacturer. I tagged along as a chef presenter. I conducted a healthy cooking demonstration, then ended up judging because some judges missed scheduled events.

The culinary competitions consisted of individuals and teams who prepared cold-food displays and hot-food cooking. I estimate that some competitors worked on their presentations for six months or more. Twenty-five teams and a host of individuals participated. Families and loved ones provided moral support, so audiences exceeded 500 people. At times, crowds were loud and animated; other times, quiet enough to hear a pin drop.

For the first time in my career, I was uncomfortable going into a show because I did not know Spanish. Chef

Claudio assured me that he would translate, but I regretted not learning a second language. I started too many times to count, but I vow to learn as it's essential for the culinary industry.

The school did a fantastic job as hosts, opening classrooms to any chefs who wanted to teach. Chef Claudio taught a couple of classes. He took command of the class, giving the students a fresh perspective from a world-class executive chef. He was in his element, speaking his native language, connecting with aspiring chefs, and making lifelong friendships. They loved it.

A celebrity in his own right, practically everyone wanted a piece of Chef Claudio, and he did his best to oblige. Socializing was one of his strengths, and he became great friends with a chef from Spain.

The Spanish chef, Chef Sebastian, taught molecular gastronomy, a food science that studies physical and chemical transformations of ingredients during cooking, at a culinary university for over twenty years. He told us that a couple of US chefs were building notoriety by bringing molecular gastronomy into their kitchens.

This man was about 6'5" and weighed over 300 pounds. He wore black-framed designer glasses, smoked like a chimney, and drank like a fish. He had a harsh raspy voice and hands that seemed too big for his body. He looked like a hitman from *The Godfather* and provided my most memorable experience of this trip.

A group of about 25 chefs went to a luncheon at a restaurant, which had been renovated and registered as a historic landmark. We arrived late enough in the afternoon that the place was almost empty. Our hosts accommodated us with a large table in the middle of the dining room. Everything was pre-set, so all we had to do was order beverages. Believe me, they had cocktails and wine aplenty. Once we settled with our beverages (mine non-alcoholic), the staff brought the food. Since the chef was the owner and a local celebrity, he made sure media was there to get photos and interviews with his esteemed guests.

One regret from my trip to Japan was that I didn't chronicle the experience. However, for this trip, I carried a pen and pad with me everywhere. With my lack of Spanish-speaking skills, and being unwilling to trouble Chef Claudio to translate, I distanced myself from most conversations. Instead, I sat back, observed, and wrote.

While we enjoyed the fellowship and meal, Chef Sebastian, who sat two seats from me, started speaking Spanish to me.

Perplexed, I nodded. *Are you talking to me?*

It took a moment for Chef Claudio to notice that I required a translator.

"He asked, 'What's the matter with you? You don't smoke or drink, and you're always writing things down? Are you trying to live forever? Are you working undercover for a secret agency? I'm scared of people like you. Life is about having fun. How are you enjoying it when you don't do anything?'"

They looked at each other. Chef Sebastian launched a boisterous laugh. They said something to each other in Spanish, looked at me, and laughed again.

I didn't ask for a translation. I let them have their moment.

Chef Sebastian directed his attention back to drinking and smoking.

To round out our trip, Chef Claudio and I visited local landmarks and networked with smaller chef groups. Although we spoke different languages, we shared the language—and love—of food. Connecting with chefs from other parts of the world increased my confidence and intensified my determination.

After returning from Ecuador, validated by almost everyone I met, I felt like I was ready for the next level. I expected my career would take off, but to my dismay…not!

I received a call from a friend who worked at a commercial kitchen equipment manufacturer group. They needed a chef, and he convinced his firm that I was their guy.

I accepted the position as company rep. I enjoyed the steady employment and consistent income—a nice change of pace. I kept my connections active and took on miscellaneous catering projects as rep jobs tend to be temporary. I didn't want the extra work, but the phone kept ringing.

I had an aggressive schedule, floating between my day job and growing my celebrity status by hustling with Mr. Thomas. As an executive with a major cable television network, he was approached with all kinds of opportunities. We grinded all hours of the day to keep momentum. We did several charitable events and pilot projects.

One of his associates needed a chef for a low-budget independent film. No financial compensation. But experience is the best teacher, and this student wanted to learn.

The horror movie, *Shadow Walkers,* was scheduled to release to DVD in the overseas market. I was responsible for feeding 50 to 80 actors and technicians including five vegans. The production ran about a month, with shooting fluctuating between mornings and evenings. Depending on the schedule, we prepared breakfast and lunch or lunch and dinner. We also had snacks available throughout the day. I wanted everything to be special; the best the crew had ever eaten. My goal was to blow them away with selection and quality.

Because we filmed in an abandoned building, dining and makeup areas were in the same space. We witnessed the lead actor's transformation to a monster. I got a sense that most of the crew had done several low-budget projects. The executive producer was the same guy who backed our Japan trip. Proximity to these professionals motivated me.

With a minimal budget, I was determined to put my signature on every meal. I convinced a good friend to throw in with me. We worked out of our make-shift kitchen at the rep group of my day job. Excitement filled me every time we loaded my car to deliver the food. The kitchen, grocery store, and production location were all within a five-mile round trip.

The crew made me feel good as they devoured everything I made. They told me that they looked forward to mealtime and took hefty portions. Most of the crew would be classified as "independent starving artists" who didn't eat as well on sets.

Editing occurred daily, and it still took about three months to finish. When the film was completed, the executive producer hosted a preview party at a local movie theater. Mostly everyone attended with families and friends. I have never been to a Hollywood movie premiere, but I cannot imagine it being any better than ours. The executive producer and director thanked everyone who contributed to the making of the film. They shared what they wanted to accomplish and how they felt about the outcome. They invited selected guests to speak about anything they felt compelled to share. We then watched the results of our efforts! Catching glimpses during production, I had no idea what to expect. To sum it up in one word: fascinating.

Following the movie, not one person left their seat. Everyone stayed through the credits to see their name on the big screen. Cheers, laughter, and crying filled the theater. I still get goosebumps thinking about it. When the house lights came up, the management team stood in front. The audience gave them a standing ovation with thunderous applause, boisterous whistling, and yelling. It seemed to last five minutes before the crowd quieted. A catered meal, complete with beer and wine, followed the showing.

What a pleasant memory. Not directly tied to my celebrity chef aspiration, the marriage of my culinary work and newly developed catering abilities was validation. I was the organizer, lead cook, transporter, manager on duty, and everything in between. Dare I say, "Well done!"

Zucchini and Eggplant Caponata

Serves 6

Many chefs are overweight, and the chefs at the national culinary show in Ecuador were no exception. As a small-framed chef who focuses on healthy food, people often assume that I cannot cook well. I prepared this Sicilian vegetarian dish during a stage demonstration as my good friend, Chef Claudio Ferrer, interpreted. May he rest in peace and power.

4 tablespoons olive oil
2 cups zucchini, small diced
2 cups eggplant, peeled and small diced
1 cup red onion, small diced
1 tablespoon garlic, minced
½ cup red pepper, small diced
½ cup green pepper, small diced
¾ cup celery, small diced
¼ cup balsamic vinegar
2 cups tomatoes, peeled, seeded and small diced
½ tablespoon oregano, chopped fine
½ tablespoon basil, chopped fine
1 tablespoon Italian parsley, chopped fine
Kosher salt and black pepper to taste
½ cup Kalamata olives, chopped fine
2 tablespoons capers, drained and rough chopped
1 cup smoked cheese (Swiss or Gouda), grated
1 package gourmet lavosh-style crackers

Heat half the oil in a large casserole or Dutch oven until medium-hot. Add zucchini and eggplant. Sauté for 5 minutes or until tender. Using a slotted spoon, remove mixture and set aside. Use remaining oil to sauté red onions until lightly browned (about 5 to 7 minutes). Add garlic, red and green peppers, and celery. Cook over low heat until all vegetables are tender (about 15 minutes), stirring occasionally. Add zucchini/eggplant mixture and vinegar to tender vegetables. Cook until well-blended. Remove pan from heat. Add tomatoes and fresh herbs. Season to taste with salt and pepper. Place in serving dish. Garnish with olives, capers, and smoked cheese. Serve with crackers.

Belize: Sink or Swim

Once I got beyond my unfulfilled expectations and returned to my daily routine as chef for a commercial kitchen equipment company, I asked myself, "What's next?" How could I get back to the magic in Japan and my ultimate dream of having my own show?

I went back to Mr. Thomas. We had planning sessions, which helped keep us motivated and focused as we worked on our individual hustles. Seemingly out of nowhere, the opportunity to film a pilot in Belize was presented.

Three to four independent companies hammered out the details and signed the contracts. The assignment was a weeklong trip to do a show that highlighted the culture, food, travel, and fun things to do in such a great country. I was designated as the host, facilitating discussions with local chefs sharing food passions and secrets with the viewing audience. The plan was to feature food trends, Belizean traditions, and spotlight local talent in other segments. Once it was finalized, it would be a pretty complete show.

Although Mr. Thomas was unable to attend, he traveled to Belize a week before us to lay the foundation for our visit. By the time we arrived, he had identified the key players, scouted possible locations, and had a good idea of the other show elements.

The lead person was a smart, savvy businessman who was transitioning into the TV and film industry. D.J. had an impressive list of projects, but this job was his first since leaving his former profession as an engineer.

The country's head of television and film was an ally in our camp. Nothing could be shot for production release without Nigel's approval. This guy was a part of our management team and part owner of the project.

The key players met for a final meeting before leaving for Belize. Mr. Thomas moderated. He round robin-ed the room, making sure everyone expressed feelings and/or concerns. We were anxious and excited to go after this tremendous opportunity. We had to succeed. No excuses. Too much rode on this project.

Other than the skilled cameraman, whom I met through Mr. Thomas, I had never worked with this crew. I was hopeful and anxious. Hopeful that they were professional, but anxious about whether I measured up. Being in front of the camera, I had no room for error. I had to be on top of my game.

Denver to Houston to Belize without a glitch. With all of the equipment, it took a while to organize. By the time we made it to customs, the closed body language—crossed arms, rolling eyes, and occasional tooth suck—of airport employees indicated that they didn't want to deal with us.

D.J., our lead man, called Nigel, the head of Belize's film department. He arrived in fifteen minutes. Like a scene from a movie, he had a quick conversation with the customs agents and voila! We were cleared and on our way.

Since it was their offseason, it was hot and speckled with a few tourists. After brief introductions with the support staff, we headed to the designated headquarters to review the itinerary. We drove to a local airport to catch puddle jumpers to our living quarters. Given the party size and weight of equipment, we needed two planes to accommodate us. We could have boated to the island; however, the trip would have taken longer because of scheduled stops. Albeit the lesser of two evils, I do not like propeller planes.

Flying on that small plane was frightening. No frills, no fuss, and no co-pilot. Nothing separated the passengers and pilot, who wore street clothes and doubled as the flight attendant. Lights flashed on the cockpit dashboard. I don't recall any communication between the pilot and control tower.

Is this an airplane seat or lawn chair?

To gain speed for takeoff, the pilot drove toward a wooded field. At the end of the runway, he turned the plane and headed toward the water. Apparently, this mode of travel was business as usual for some passengers. They were cool, calm, and collected. My heart jumped in my throat and stayed there the duration of the flight. For about 35 minutes, I clinched the seat and prayed for traveling mercies. Completely unnerved upon landing, I thanked God for a solid foundation...land!

Before I could kiss the ground and breathe a sigh of relief, Nigel instructed us to gather the gear and luggage for the boat ride.

As if my newfound fear of small planes wasn't bad enough, my fear of water is insurmountable in comparison. Other than cooking and bathing, I do not mess with water. I was ready to cry.

Again exceeding weight limits, we split into two groups. How dare they plop me on a water taxi. The oversized row boats with high-powered motors mounted on the back whizzed everywhere. To add fuel to the fire, each jalopy was operated by one person who stood near the motor. No backup crew or alternative course of action in the event the captain abandoned the sinking ship. I tried to play it cool, but on the inside, I trembled. *Please don't look at or speak to me.*

I'm in need of a doctor. Please, GOD, don't let anything happen to me. Fear gripped me so tightly that I don't remember how long that boat ride took.

I praised God for placing my feet on solid ground. It took a few minutes to calm my nerves when Nigel announced the next boat would arrive shortly.

Wait! What? I almost lost control of my bladder.

More crew members joined us on the dock. They had casual conversations, while I stood alone. I was too scared and pissed. Why did they station us in the boonies? Had I known the expedition to uncharted territories would have put me in front of my two greatest fears, I would've stayed home. I had no intention of ever confronting these fears.

During the second boat ride, I shut down again. Except for praying, I did not have words for anyone.

When we docked, the midnight black sky was filled with bright stars. I remember because I looked up at God to express gratitude. "Are we there yet, or should I expect another boat?"

Ambergris Caye is an island off the east coast of Belize that sets in the Caribbean Sea. Our destination was the northern part of the island near the Mexican border. With tourism as its main industry, I had never seen natural beauty of this magnitude. White sandy beaches for miles and crystal clear blue water. With a break about two miles out, a gentle wave rolled into shore. Exclusive resort properties lined the beachfront, looking like majestic castles.

First-class units from three different owners were available to us. We had to figure out lodging assignments, which was an involved ordeal because multiple crews were slated for various destinations. To minimize production time and cost, teams had to work independently to film content to create a cohesive show.

Steve Roberts, the cameraman, and I stayed in the same suite. We figured spending time together would create familiarity and comfortability that would reflect in the content.

When I walked into the unit of the privately-owned villa, I said to myself, "The journey was totally worth it." The luxury accommodations included beautifully decorated bedrooms, a full kitchen, and all the comforts of home. The spectacular beach-front view was perfect for sunset watching and star gazing. Relaxing on a hammock on the enclosed porch…bliss.

Steve unpacked, cleaned, and charged his equipment. He linked the system together to download captured content while we slept.

I unpacked my equipment…uniforms. I ironed my clothes. I'm a fanatic about my appearance, especially when filming. Since most of my projects had been little to no budget, I doubled as my stylist and enjoyed it. I used the time to gather my thoughts and visualize what I needed to do. I took three to four hours to prep wardrobe for two days of filming.

Steve and I walked about a mile along the beach to have breakfast with the crew at the resort, which served as headquarters. The nontraditional spread included fresh-out-the-water seafood and fresh-off-the-vine fruit including pineapples, mangos, papayas, and other indigenous fruit. I didn't waste stomach space eating bread or pastries.

We discussed crew assignments and scheduling, which took longer than expected because we had never worked together. To expedite the process, the producer and director decided the shoot schedules and roles.

The director said, "Strap in, boys! These next few days will hit us like a hurricane."

With such an aggressive schedule, crews had to divide and conquer. Some of us stayed on location to film aspects of the resort, while others went to the mainland.

Feeling like we were already behind, Steve and I were anxious to get started. We had three assistants, and our five-man team became good friends. A combination of excitement and nervousness fueled us to go, go, and go. The first day was a long mental grind, but we made up for lost time and got ahead of schedule.

The challenge was factoring in footage from the other crews to envision the project. It was like putting together a jigsaw puzzle without seeing all the pieces. Since the producer and director were with the other crew, we had to make decisions on our own. What artist doesn't like creative freedom? We developed our rhythm, and the show evolved.

On occasion, we went to Hotel Protofino Beach Resort, our designated headquarters, to regroup and focus. The resort staff were fantastic people, as nice as nice could be. They provided us with everything we needed to run at maximum efficiency: food, supplies, computer access, etc. In return, we did extensive filming there, giving them top exposure and free publicity. A win-win for all parties.

Being a coastal country, much of the Belizean lifestyle revolves around water. If this trip was going to be a success, I had to face my fear of water, and I only had a few days to do it.

During the summers, the City of Detroit provided swim mobiles—converted semi-trailers—for inner-city kids. Six rigs traveled to various neighborhoods as free swimming pools so kids would not open fire hydrants for cool fun.

The swim mobile had lots of steps that opened to a platform that circled the pool. The platform was separated into sections that correlated to water depths with six feet being the deepest. A lifeguard stood at each end of the pool.

I wanted to do everything my older siblings did, but at six or seven, I was too young to participate. I watched from the curb.

When I mustered the nerve to get in the pool, I was supposed to go to the shallow section. But in the midst of the chaos of kids, I got separated from LaGreta and Roger. I had no idea what I was doing. As I wandered around, an excited kid pushed me into water above my head. Panic. I couldn't swim. I thought I was drowning. I splashed and flailed, gasping for air. Thank God someone rescued me. I was told that they did chest compressions until I coughed up water and started breathing. I didn't get into a body of water bigger than a bathtub until Belize.

Our shooting schedule had us visiting several beaches, which meant getting in the boat. Water, water, everywhere.

The boat captain, a relative of a crew member, was a cross between Robert Redford's character in the 1998 film, *The Horse Whisperer*, and Fred Sanford of the '70s sitcom, *Sanford and Son*. He stood about 6' 2" tall with dark sunbaked skin, dreads to the middle of his back, broad shoulders, rugged hands, and a huge smile. With a fat joint dangling in his mouth, he wore a long-sleeved white shirt, turquoise swim trunks, and a knitted hat. I'm a sucker for accents, and I enjoyed his. I dubbed him "Fish Whisperer" because he had a way with the water and its creatures.

His boat would have been at home in Fred Stanford's junkyard. Looking fifty years old, it had ten colors of patchwork metal and tons of hanging decorations. Bob Marley music blared from an old boom box. His two-man crew was non-descript, locals who seemed to be along to have a good time.

As the garbage barge, I mean boat pulled into the dock, I said to myself, "No way I'm getting on that thing." It didn't look sturdy enough to support me without sinking, let alone a full production crew.

On the deck of the boat, we discussed details for the shoot. I overheard Fish Whisperer's relative tell him to put on a show for the cameras to promote his business.

Fish Whisperer tapped Steve on the shoulder. "Excuse me for one second. I need you to follow me." He grabbed a small fish from a bucket, walked to the back of the boat, and held the fish in the air. "Get your cameras ready." He put the fish in his mouth and tilted his head back. A bird swooped down and plucked it out of his mouth!

Stunned, I said to myself, "Who is this guy?"

He did it a few more times to make sure the cameraman had good angles and coverage.

After his exhibition, we returned to the front of the boat to continue the pre-shoot meeting.

Fish Whisperer said, "Hold on a second." He took off his hat and shirt and dove in the water.

"What the—"

Three minutes later, he emerged with a nice-sized squid wrapped around his arm. He brought it on board, grabbed a white five-gallon bucket, and removed the squid from his arm. Once the squid was in the bucket, he grabbed a knife. "Watch out!" He pricked the squid to release its black ink. He looked up at us with his gigantic smile. "This is gonna be some good eating."

The crew laughed. They got a big kick out of him and his antics.

He laughed. "I looked down, saw it, and had to go get it. I figured it was a sign of great things ahead for today."

I freaked out. We hadn't left the dock and Jacques Cousteau was retrieving creatures from the depths of the sea.

A crew member must have seen the fear on my face. "Don't worry, there's no one on the island like him. He'll get us the best action on the water today."

"Uh huh." Although I feared for my life, I was not going to let a little H_2O stop my dreams. *Lord, please don't let this be a three-hour tour to Gilligan's Island.*

As we prepared the boat, one of the guys handed me a fresh coconut. "Would you like some? I'm sure you haven't had anything like it before."

I took a small sip and then guzzled the rest. Good and quite refreshing.

Fish Whisperer moved around the boat, laughing, joking, and doing his thing. Within five minutes of setting sail, he dove off the side. He came out of the water with two lobsters. "Man, I saw a bunch of them down there and couldn't pass them up."

I cooked lots of lobster but never witnessed hand-caught protein.

He climbed onto the boat. Instead of drying off with a towel, he let the sun bake off the water. He slid back into his busy routine of captaining this unique vessel.

Realizing this guy was an expert who knew what he was doing, I relaxed a little. I'm sure he mastered his craft hands-on versus a degree or formal training. My admiration for him grew leaps and bounds as the day unfolded.

He took command of the boat. "Hey, guys. We're going to change this up. I want to show you some stingrays." He pointed to the right side of the boat—port or starboard, I don't know. "They're over there."

I didn't see anything. "What are you talking about? How do you know there's stingray there?" It's great to be in the presence of an expert operating in their expertise.

Fish Whisperer was conversing with his guy in a dialect I couldn't understand and then he yelled, "Come here!"

We all ran to him.

He pointed. "Look down. There they are!"

Swimming alongside the boat were about seventy stingrays. These creatures were gray on top, white on bottom, and had a wingspan of almost five feet.

Fish Whisperer barked out commands, and the boat slowed. "This is the spot right here."

The crew anchored and secured the boat so we could capture footage from the deck and underwater.

The captain called us together. "Here's how we're going to do this." He gave his crew instructions, and they went into action. He instructed us on water safety, how to interact with the stingrays, then dove into the water. In a few minutes, a fever of stingrays surrounded him. He bobbed in the water with a huge smile. "Come on in."

One of the guides took off his clothes and dove in. He surfaced with a smile as wide as Fish Whisperer's. "Come on in. What are you waiting for?"

I know he's not talking to me.

A guide, who was still in his right mind standing on the deck of the boat, said, "Keith, are you going to get in?"

"No! I'm afraid of water."

"Hey, there's nothing wrong with being afraid, but in this water, there's nothing to be afraid of. The water is calm. You can stand in it, and you won't be underwater."

"What about you? Are you going in?"

"Nope, not today." He sighed. "I don't feel well, so I'm trying to take it easy."

"Hope you feel better." I looked down into the water and then backed away from the side of the boat.

He teased me, trying to push my pride button. "You came all the way down here and won't get in the water? Those stingrays don't care about you. Chicken!"

This friendly game got under my skin. The subtle pushing worked my nerves.

"We need this shot for the show, and you won't give it to us because you're scared." His look of disgust was all telling.

Embarrassed, I said, "Okay. Enough already. I'm going in!" I took off my shirt and pants. I had on swim trunks as a just-in-case fashion statement to saunter in the safety and security of the beach, not actual water play. No head-first entry for me. I climbed down the ladder.

I must have been a comical sight because everyone laughed without restraint.

My breathing became quick and heavy as I waded to the group petting the stingrays.

One of them said, "Do you care to pet Betsy? Be gentle and stroke her like this."

I took a minute to process that I was standing in the Caribbean Sea. I was glad that it was being filmed, so I had indisputable proof of overcoming my aquatic fear. The longer I stayed in the water, the more comfortable I became. My breathing relaxed and softened. I stopped panicking. I waded to the stingrays and pet Betsy! An experience of a lifetime.

The assistant and I got back on the boat. The Fish Whisperer spent a little more time in the water and then returned to the boat. With a wide smile, he glistened from the sun.

I started the day nervous, worried, and scared when the man with the piece-of-crap boat, old shoes, and tattered clothes pulled up to the dock. By the end of the day, I had conquered a lifelong fear and made new friends. Lesson: people make judgments based on appearances and many times they're wrong. Fish Whisperer looked penniless, but he was one of the richest men I had ever met. He made a lasting impression on me, and I aspire to follow his mantra: live a free life.

We had one incredible experience after another in Belize. The visit concluded with my participation in the national holiday: Garifuna Settlement Day. Observed on November 19th, the holiday celebrates the settlement of the Garifuna people in Belize after exile from the Grenadines by the British. It's equivalent to Independence Day in the US. The festivities include a parade with street music, dancing, and fabulous food.

The celebration started in the heart of the city at their national church. The service was standing room only with a gathering of people waiting outside. After service, the elders and city dignitaries started a procession from the pulpit. The doors swung open, musicians played, and folks sang. The lineup was respectful and orderly as the outside crowd waited for everyone in the church to get set before they joined the processional.

We marched to the city park. The line, eclipsing more than two miles, accommodated participants in festive costumes. The funky music had a reggae-jazz vibe. Either in the "Conga line," hanging out of windows, or dancing on the sidewalks, no one sat in lawn chairs waiting to be entertained. They recognized me as a celebrity and invited me to join the fun. I had a ball partying with them, and the film crew caught it all.

The celebration escalated at the park. The church elders walked onto the stage to start the program. People separated into smaller groups, engaging in jovial conversations with laughter and smiles aplenty.

The crew went to the area with food vendors for the contest. Designated judges tasted and evaluated items to award prizes. The crew was not shy about letting festival guests know that I was a celebrity chef from the United States. That bit of information motivated would-be chefs to invite me to try their food even if they weren't participating in the contest. Their faces lit up when I asked them to explain their dish.

A guy handed me a bowl of food. "You've got to try this. It's the best on the island. A family recipe passed down through the years."

I took a small sample to assess the flavor and ingredients. The vendor smiled and proudly nodded, thrilled that I tasted his food. Its flavor reminded me of rabbit.

Pulu, my escort, was a local legend as a former basketball player. He ran to me. "Chef, you're eating gibnut stew! We call that the royal rat!" He released a boisterous laugh.

I almost spit out the food.

Pulu explained that Queen Elizabeth was served this delicacy during a visit to the island. The meat was paca, a large rat-like rodent with dots and stripes on the sides, short ears, and a tiny tail. It tasted like gamey ham or greasy rabbit.

I calmed down a little and gave away the rest of the stew. I asked the escort to translate to the vendor that I need to pace myself because I have lots of food to try.

As vendors got into their explanations, their pride took over. They became more vocal and animated in their descriptions. A few of them were so expressive it made me more excited to taste what they had. I think their excitement made the dish taste better. In the midst of sampling food, I noticed two distinct dynamics.

Homeless people tried to get what they could from the party revelers. They weren't at all bashful. Some of them acted as if we owed them something. They demanded that we give them money. They did whatever they had to do to live: beg, steal, prostitute.

The second dynamic dealt with food. Given my background, I always reference execution. What did you do to set up? I start with safety, considering my friends from the Health Department. Often deemed a necessary evil, caterers do what inspectors say because they have the power to shut down food service. The system is in place to eliminate food poisoning.

Well, outside at a Belize park, the food vendors were big-time catering. I didn't see any Health Department staff, anywhere, checking on anything. I wondered if I was being the "ugly American," assuming our values, systems, and rules were the best in the world. With each tasted dish, I worried about proper refrigeration, temperature monitoring, sanitation, and proper storage. I saw little, if any, of these safety measures. My mind raced thinking about the bad things that could happen by eating this "unauthorized food." Where were the coolers, ice, and refrigeration? Where were the chafing dishes and ovens to keep hot food hot?

I'm not eating anything else. I cannot afford to get sick.

When we walked to a booth, the chef had a huge smile and was ready to give me a sample. I felt their pride. The vendors expressed appreciation and said that my brief visit brought them honor. My American attitude and training were null and void.

Come on, Keith. Let your guard down and accept them as they have you.

I calmed my fears. Instead of a hardline stance on food tasting, I took a lighter approach and played up the irony of lax standards. I flowed with the exchanges until I met a homeless kid. He followed me for a while and then touched me, smiled, and ran away.

I smiled, waved, and kept visiting booths.

He watched me from a distance. He eventually walked over to me, touched me again, and stood there.

I was speaking with a chef, sampling his food and learning how it's made. I know that my stomach isn't big enough to taste everyone's food, and I didn't want to be disrespectful by trying some dishes and not others. Lightbulb moment. I'll sample it all. Whatever I don't eat, I'll give to my new friend.

Little did I know, my new friend came with a mom and two siblings. When I gave him food, he gave it to his mother. She came up to me and happily accepted my leftovers. When others tried to jump on the bandwagon, the crew stopped it because the hungry crowd was impeding their ability to film.

My heart broke for this family living in rampant poverty. *What do they do when there's no holiday?* These kids should have been in school, but they're learning hard life lessons on the streets. Imagine the juxtaposition of celebration and poverty side by side. Humbled and honored for the recognition but sick to my stomach at the horrible conditions. Innocent victims. All children deserve a chance to be the best that they can be.

I kept giving the family food. I loved their smiles.

A crew member tapped me on the shoulder. "Slow your roll, chef. I know this family. They live in the park, along with several families who make it through by begging."

"Really?"

"Yeah. The mother is a druggie and an alcoholic."

Another crew member moved close to me. "You can't save 'em. I know it hurts to hear that, but we have a job to do. Get your head back in the game."

It took me a few minutes to regain my composure.

The celebration went into the night and through the next day. We got great footage and created lasting memories. We packed as my adopted family waved goodbye. With those long faces, I thought about their bleak futures. Another life lesson: be happy. As long as you wake above the dirt, you're blessed.

We moved to other areas of the city to capture content for other segments. I wrestled with our resort living and the poverty of locals. I assume parts of town were ritzy with folks living well, but poverty prevailed.

When our stay at the plush villa ended, we packed to stay at a friend's apartment in the city. As we said our goodbyes, some of the folks said that they thought I was an arrogant, conceited TV guy because I didn't look at or speak to any of them. I confessed my fear of water and apologized.

When we settled into the new living quarters, my cameraman downloaded content. I went to the patio, laid on the hammock, and tried to decompress. My mind raced with the stark differences between tourists and locals, country laws and norms. I drifted off to a pleasant sleep, exhausted from the day's mental anguish.

A few hours later, a couple of the crew and I decided to get a quick bite to eat. As we strolled down the street, we came across kids—I guess middle school age—walking. They wore school uniforms and toted backpacks.

One of the boys looked at me. "Hey! You're the guy I saw on TV last night."

"You're right. That was me."

Excited, he said, "Can you wait right here? I want to go get someone."

"Sure. We don't have anything to do."

He raced back with a friend and introduced us. "This is the guy I saw on TV last night. He's a famous chef filming a TV show."

We spoke for a couple of minutes, and they asked for my autograph. As classmates passed by, the two young men smiled. They puffed their chests and nodded as if to say, "Yeah, this is my friend."

To have that effect on someone is incredible. I don't take this blessing and my responsibility lightly. I saw the young man a couple more times. Each time, he introduced me to whoever was with him. He said that he wanted to be a famous chef like me. I'm hopeful that he'll make his dream come true.

While the recognition was great, I wanted to master the behind-the-scenes process. I had the opportunity to work with the project's decision makers: the director and Belize's minister of TV and film. I learned how to critique a show by answering these questions: What results do the brains and backers want? How do they evaluate footage and decide how to bring it together?

They loved my work in front of the camera: engaging guests, inspiring chefs, connecting with the audience. The only negative comment was that, with so much great content, I made their jobs harder. If the byproduct of giving my best is resounding results and glowing reviews, I can live with the outcome. Dare I say, "Well done!"

We decided to split the footage between Belize and the US since crews in each location were responsible for various aspects of the show. Locked and loaded with our plan, we relaxed for the rest of the day. We had an early flight the next morning.

At the airport, a female officer said in a rather loud voice, "Hey, I recognize you. You're that famous chef from TV. You came here to film another show, right? Can we take a picture together?"

I was done...well done. God watched out for me and blessed me in ways that I didn't understand. Although I put in intense work days, I got on the plane energized. With yet another confirmation, I walked away knowing that I could do TV and bring value.

I pray that I am chosen to work with experts whose skills keep me humble and hunger keeps me motivated. My approach will always be the same: Keith, you must get better. As I grow my brand, this blessing will follow. I must be so good that my work speaks for itself.

Belizean Fry Jacks

Makes 10 fry jacks

While filming *Taste of Belize*, we had these delicious fry jacks for breakfast. This dish served with fresh fruit, seafood, and cheeses was a tremendous start to a successful day.

3 cups all-purpose flour
2 teaspoons baking powder
1 teaspoon salt
1 tablespoon shortening
1 cup water
2 cups vegetable oil for frying

Mix flour, baking powder, and salt into a bowl. Cut shortening into flour. Slowly add water and mix to make a soft, non-sticky dough. Divide dough in half and let rest for 15-20 minutes. Flour countertop or board. Roll dough in circles 10-20 inches in diameter. Cut into 3-inch strips and then cut crosswise to create small triangles. Fry each side in hot oil until golden brown.

Note: Use 350-365° oil to ensure the jacks puff up. If you do not have an oil thermometer, toss a pinch of flour into the oil. If it sizzles, you're good to go; however, if it browns immediately, then the oil is too hot. For a crunchier texture and to prevent puffing, put a small slit in the dough pieces before frying.

Keith Denard Jones

Just Keep Grinding

After Belize, I was hopeful that my path would be a little easier, but once again, I had to keep grinding. I didn't have a restaurant where I was accessible to the public, so how would folks know me?

I landed jobs that helped pay bills or increased my budding celebrity chef brand. I knew people would be my path to success. When God put a person in my life, I asked two questions: Why are they here? How can we help each other advance? My commitment never wavered. I had heart-to-hearts with myself to put what I accomplished into perspective. I made progress, but instead of celebrating the small successes, I focused on what needed to be done.

With perpetual changes in this volatile industry, the hate was consistent. Some people are proficient at destroying dreams and demolishing destinies. Instead of using their actions as an excuse to quit, I used it as fuel to propel me. Naysayers kept me focused, alert, and ready to adapt.

I had conversations with God to analyze why things hadn't happened by a certain time. What else did I need to do or prove to get where I wanted to be? I reminded myself that this journey is a marathon, not a sprint. My job is to trust Him, put action behind my faith, and develop my professional and personal skills. Live and learn the lessons. To whom much is given, much is expected. God was preparing me to be a total package. I had to be patient, humble, and true.

My food-on-the-table job kept me busy as my hustle-to-celebrity-status moved forward. I worked for the major equipment company on out-of-state jobs, but I was not a company man. I was too far from my purpose and too independent. We tolerated one another. It could have been a great partnership. They provide me with money and resources, and I generate multiplied returns on their investment. But I could not convince them to give me an audience with the decision makers to share my vision.

Why should they get behind me when they had a corporate chef and company objectives? Any time I spent growing their vision, put me further behind on my own. In good conscience, I could not advance my agenda on their dime. Unethical. Since I could not effectively represent them and myself, integrity told me to walk away. I needed to replace the income, so I looked for opportunities.

After a few months of trying to balance my food-on-the-table job, celebrity-chef-brand-building hustle, and confliction about which to support, I prayed. I didn't ask for a monumental miracle, just a small blessing to keep my machine running.

Like Tiger Woods said during a golf tournament, "At some point, I just have to keep grinding away. Everything doesn't always work the way I want, so I have to stay close and grind. Keep at it and give myself a chance."

My success or failure is based on me. No excuses, no one to blame…only myself.

One day, as I drove to a private catering event, I got a phone call. The person on the other end worked for a local production company. He wanted to interview me. We confirmed the appointment for the next day. My initial thought was, *I'm getting punked*.

I did a little homework. The company was one of the largest players in the Food TV game. Excited and cautious, I pondered how they found me.

I contacted Mr. Thomas. He advised me on how he would approach the opportunity. I relaxed and developed a plan. You only get one chance to make a first impression, so I was going to wow them from start to finish. My goal was to nail the interview.

The private catering event was a blur that seemed to go on forever. I had trouble focusing. Jitters stole my appetite.

I ironed my outfit, polished my shoes, and assembled accessories: watch, bracelet, and leather briefcase for my resume. I guess my excitement and nervousness settled overnight. Driving to the interview, I sang with the radio and thought about my family. Everything I did was for them. They inspired and motivated me to do my best.

I arrived a bit too early and had to wait in the lobby of the secured facility. About ten minutes later, an attractive young lady escorted me to Mr. G.'s office.

Although this meeting had the power to change my life, I remained calm. We shook hands and exchanged business cards.

He provided some background on himself. "Let me take you on a tour of our facility. We can have the interview when we come back to my office. I have about an hour and fifteen minutes before my next appointment, so I'm hoping we can get this done by then."

"That sounds fine to me."

They were a full-service production company, outfitted with a small studio, green screen rooms, and about eight editing bays. The space included private offices, a lunchroom, kitchen, and a massive office area separated into one-person cubicles.

"We've outgrown the space. Our new home should be ready within a year. In addition to increased square footage, it'll have more production studios and other amenities to make us more self-contained and efficient." He shared inside information.

I loved every moment.

We returned to his office.

"We have an excellent track record of providing TV show content to the largest food network in television."

I nodded.

"As a matter of fact, we have an agreement which states that any food program we produce must be pitched to them first."

"Impressive."

"We've been so successful bringing them shows that I can predict with 85-90% certainty whether they will green light a new idea. It's not a matter of if, but how many they order to launch it."

Calm down, breathe, count to five. As every fiber of my being shook, I never let him see me sweat. I fielded his questions with ease.

After some general questions, he asked about my childhood, family, and culinary background. I understood the latter, but my upbringing? How did that play into a TV show? I gave him the abridged version.

"If you could design your own show, what would it look like?"

I took my time explaining my vision.

His facial expressions spoke volumes. He remained silent for several seconds.

"Interesting idea. Don't know if it could be a weekly show, but a one-hour special is possible."

I sighed. This idea bubbled inside me for years, and he blew it up in an instant. I rolled with the disappointment and killed the rest of the interview, which was more like a casual conversation between friends.

Mr. G. said, "Do you have any questions for me?"

"Yes, sir. Only one. Can you tell me how you found me?"

"I have a team of people assigned to search the web for content. They came across your videos, did a little more research, and I decided to call."

At the conclusion of the interview, he said, "Thanks for coming in. Let me figure out a few things and talk with my team. I'll get back to you."

"Great. I look forward to hearing from you."

"It'll take me a few days, but I promise to let you know something either way." He walked me to the main entrance.

I waved goodbye, happy to have made another connection with an influencer. I recapped the exchange on the drive home. I was satisfied with my responses. I thanked God and continued my day.

Two days later, I got a call as I pulled into my driveway. Without looking at the caller ID, I answered the phone. "Good afternoon. This is Keith. How can I help you?"

"Keith, good afternoon. This is Mr. G. I have great news. I am officially in the Keith Jones business! My team and I will be working 24/7 on a show for you until we nail a concept. You have what it takes: talent and personality. It's our job to flesh that out and create a show for you.

"That's wonderful. Thank you. What do you need from me?"

"I have a two-week family vacation and then need a week to catch up. In about three weeks, I'll call you to get you back in here to meet the team. We're going to have a great time working together."

I pinched myself three times. "Thank you so much for your call and belief in me. I look forward to getting started."

After years of hard work, God had opened the windows, doors, and roof. My culinary life flashed before my eyes. I recalled the wins and losses. Although the journey wasn't easy, it was worth it. I cried. I sat in the car to regain my composure before walking into the house.

My family, who felt my joy, pain, and disappointment, had experienced enough ebbs and flows, so I decided to keep this news to myself until it moved along.

For the next few days, I was in a fog, trying to contain my excitement and function as normal. All I thought about was that phone call!

Two days, seven hours, and thirty-two minutes past the three-week point, Mr. G. had not called.

I called him.

"Keith, I purposely avoided calling you. I don't agree with my boss's decision, but I'm officially out of the Keith Jones business."

Shocked, crushed, and deflated. "Are you kidding me? What happened?"

"I was so excited that I sent your materials to my boss in New York. I wanted to let her know we found our next talent. She looked at it and said, 'He's nothing special. We'll pass.'"

I sighed.

"I must apologize to you. I should've waited until we developed the concept and then sent that to her. What I sent wasn't a true representation of your talent. I'm pissed because you have everything we need and more. We spend a great deal of time and resources looking for people like you, and she tells me 'He's nothing special.' I was so upset I wanted to quit. As much as I want to move forward with you, I can't stick out my neck."

I fought to keep it together. This decision wasn't on him, so I did my best to console him.

"Don't give up on your dream, Keith. You have as much, if not more, talent than many of the folks currently on the network. You have the 'it' factor."

His boss's words cut like a knife. I fell into a funk. I didn't want to hear, think, or see anything about TV. I went about my daily life trying to manage yet another crushing blow. For three weeks, I wallowed in pity because I allowed the haters to inject me with self-doubt. I pondered: Am I not cut out for this? What is it about me that makes people say "no"? What do I need to do? I'm so glad I spared my family from the agony of defeat.

Once I processed through the rejection and evaluated the lesson, I learned something about myself. I am a genuine optimist. I developed a thicker skin, turned that rejection into motivation, and used it to fuel my resolve. I alone determine my fate. I refuse to give my power to anyone else.

After five years of sporadic employment, dream chasing, and jacked up credit, I had an uneasy feeling. I had a conversation with God and, once again, He provided. Without looking, I landed a full-time job. The transition from where-will-my-next-paycheck-come-from to weekly paydays was smooth.

I was hired by a food manufacturer to develop recipes for home and professional chefs using their products. The owner wanted me to create video support materials, which included recipes, TV commercials, and training on how to sell products.

The owner and I met at a Denny's a couple of times to put together my program and compensation package. Just like that, I killed two birds with one stone: accomplish his goals and keep my dream alive. Unlike a corporation with decision-makers across the country, I worked directly with the owner, founder of the company. He wanted me to learn all aspects of the business to be ready to function in another capacity. I immersed myself into his business.

I was excited to work with a new team and hopeful to make lasting friendships. Failure was not an option, so I got my butt in gear, learned the nuances, and kept my learning curve short. As my own worst critic, I wanted to know the business better than him. No more freelancing or winging it. I was an employee who had to adjust to 9-to-5 hours, answering to the boss and his office manager.

I showed up the first day confident. I met with the owner and staff. Before lunch, I realized that the transition would not be as smooth as I expected.

A dose of hate spewed from the office manager. I don't know if she thought I wanted her job or she was just mean because it was Monday, but I felt her negative energy.

After the blatant disrespect, I found out that the owner wanted me to manage existing accounts and get new ones.

What? I'm not a salesperson. What happened to creating recipes and all that we discussed? Having many first days, I reserve my evaluation of the staff; however, this first day was different. I tried to break the barrier to get beyond the hate. I got nothing. The owner left me to figure out things as he built his business.

Throughout my career, I met salespeople who used to be chefs. I did not want to be one of them. I looked down on them, assuming the kitchen was too hot, so they got out of it. *Hate and sales on my first day. You've got to be kidding me.* I was conflicted between returning to the grind and a steady paycheck.

I developed new skills to be successful at this job. I learned the unique production process, supply chain management, and mastered sales strategies.

In the beginning, I dealt with the hate by ignoring it. My initial assumption was racism; however, I soon realized that she was an equal-opportunity hater. Age, race, and gender didn't matter to her. At some point, every employee felt her venomous wrath. I didn't have the power to remove the hater, so I dealt with her antics on a case-by-case basis. I documented everything I did to have an arsenal of proof when she claimed I made an error. I didn't have control over her hate, but I did have control over how I responded.

As for the sales, I chose to learn and became consumed with its psychology and methodology. The owner was very specific about how he wanted to take his product to market and did not want any deviation. To complicate matters, we had two divisions, retail and wholesale, which went to market on different paths.

Given the desired outcomes, you would think that formal training would be provided. Not! My learning curve was riddled with ebbs and flows on the self-guided training. Having the hate of a key employee glaring at me served to complicate things.

She went out of her way to make things difficult. Not only was dysfunction rampant with this employee, dysfunction funneled throughout the staff. Having built numerous successful teams, I knew that I could shift this dynamic; however, the effort required was more than I could spare. I had to master the business and then address the people issues.

I had to prove my worth every minute of every day; otherwise, the hater brought it to the owner's attention. That cold-and-calculating person had no sympathy. When I needed assistance, most employees provided answers. But the hater? Never. Not only did she refuse to help, she took every opportunity to sabotage me. She dropped the hammer from the beginning and did nothing to help me acclimate. Nevertheless, I had other fish to fry.

With the resistance, it took a few months to build my foundation and get comfortable in the job. I enjoyed learning. The challenge was refreshing. I came to work excited with a little pep in my step, happy to be a part of this new company.

I was in position to implement my you-are-only-as-good-as-your-crew philosophy to build a fantastic team. However, the hater had erected an impenetrable fortress, and I ran smack into it without coming close to building a cohesive team. Because of the company's culture, employees had an every-man-for-himself mentality. No team spirit, group synergy, or camaraderie. We stumbled into working together; however, we never maximized our potential.

The owner gave me more responsibilities, and I gained confidence as a salesman. In the midst of thistles and thorns, I blossomed. The more the job required, the more I gave.

Three salespeople and a supervisor made up the wholesale team. After a brief training, the supervisor, who worked directly with the owner and our largest customer, moved to the retail division. I had full responsibility for the wholesale sales team.

Although he was a professional salesperson, I soon realized that my predecessor did minimal work while projecting maximum effort. Unwilling to rat him out and with more pressing needs vying for my attention, I let his work ethic speak for itself.

Our largest customer had locations across the United States. They required ongoing tasting samples and demos at selected stores. Mr. Retail oversaw this program, which didn't require much management. Once the schedule was set, two crews of three people executed the demos with minimal input from the supervisor. A sweet setup.

With limited knowledge and no direction on how the owner wanted sales to grow, I considered myself the weakest link. But I knew people and how to motivate them. It took a little time for the wholesale team to become comfortable with me and each another. Two of the guys tried to trick me into thinking they were working hard. I let them know in no uncertain terms that I recognized game. Nothing personal, strictly business. Once I established boundaries, everyone got to work and our sales grew.

Given my predecessor was a work minimalist, room for improvement was limitless. On the climb to growth, I butted heads with team members on occasion. I did not show any weakness, and to their credit, they rolled with my changes.

I spent most of my time with the newest team member, simultaneously teaching and learning. I split the country into three regions—North, South, and West—and assigned a member to each. It took about three months to develop a rhythm.

A key element to sales success is the ability to develop relationships. I instructed my team to connect with the folks who helped us meet our objectives. Mr. S., an associate in the wholesale division, pushed me to allow him to visit his accounts to "build rapport and boost customer satisfaction." What he actually wanted was to have a good time with the company's time and dime. He wanted to eat, drink, and entertain his customers while chasing women. Outside of a paycheck, his only purpose was going outside to play.

Do as you please in your personal time, but in the real world, where we work for a living, his logic was flawed. Why jeopardize solid employment?

Once I get comfortable in my job, I'll clean up all this crap. Although my primary responsibilities were on the wholesale side, I spent time learning the retail side. I wanted a real clear picture of how both sides of the business were supposed to operate. I got it.

After a while, I felt much better because I wasn't just earning my keep; I was adding value. I executed projects and got measurable results on both sides of the business despite the hate and negativity. The more I did, the more I learned. My reward: more responsibilities. The owner learned to trust me.

"Keith, I'd like for you to make decisions in my absence, so I need you to learn how I think and operate."

After about nine months of flowing together, the owner called me into his office.

"The cost of raw materials has been escalating over the past couple months. I'm very concerned. I thought about letting some people go because we can't afford to absorb these increases much longer."

"Okay. Let me know if there's anything I can do to help." I must have had the oh-Lord-is-my-job-at-risk look.

"Not to worry. I really need you, but if these prices keep climbing, I'll have to close down the sales department."

Armed with this new information, I checked in with the sales team. They asked if their jobs were in jeopardy.

"Absolutely not." I had to avoid the tsunami of fleeing salespeople and the effect of employee turnover to the customer. Although we were in trouble, my job required me to steady anxiety. I tried to assure them that the owner and I discussed future growth, not layoffs.

Unable to maintain his composure, the owner stressed out more. Minor issues became catastrophic.

My team sensed something was wrong. "What's going on? Will we be fired?"

For two months, I kept it under wraps. But after the owner put it out there, I had to explain who was losing their job.

Another management issue was availability. Between man-made and natural disasters, we couldn't get our raw product. Lack of supply caused prices to shoot through the roof. Because we had demand, we'd gladly pay the inflated price, but stock was so limited that we couldn't get any. Supply and demand, a double whammy.

The owner freaked out often and in the open.

I felt sick to my stomach. Although my position was "safe," my sales team was on the chopping block. I was the last one hired, so shouldn't I be the first one fired?

The retail supervisor was all about self-preservation. He felt the hammer coming and positioned himself on the stay side of stay or go.

The owner called me to a secluded office only used when he didn't want anyone to hear conversations.

"Keith, I can't go on like this. I have to make changes. I'm thinking about a significant pay cut for you and letting the sales team go."

"I knew this day was coming. Instead of a pay cut, give me two weeks to find another job."

"No. I don't want to lose you. Let's see if we can work out something?"

"I can't see everyone else go, especially since I was the last person hired."

"Keith, you offer me so much more. I don't look at you like I look at them. You're indispensable and irreplaceable."

"Thanks for the compliment. Please give me time to find something and I'll be gone. I watched you agonize over options for the past few months. I understand your situation and know that you've done all you can. This situation isn't on you. You're a generous and honorable man who's been more than fair to us."

"Let's just see what happens over the next two weeks?"

"Okay." In my mind, I was already gone.

Frustrated that I had paused my dream for the one-year temporary position, I had a hard time pulling myself together. What am I going to do now? Was I wrong to walk away from all that I had built? Albeit sporadic, it was mine.

Having seen the handwriting on the wall, I had curated a list of contacts with job prospects. On the first phone call, I landed a job paying a little more. #Blessed.

I notified my staff that I had turned in my resignation notice. I hoped my early departure would buy them more time.

Almost unanimously, they said, "If you're gone, we don't stand a chance." They went into self-preservation mode and made calls.

I did what I could to help them get other jobs.

The retail supervisor's responsibilities required him to travel out of state. He took his laptop to keep up with business. On one of the trips, his computer locked up; he couldn't do anything with it. When he returned to the office, he was consumed with getting it fixed.

"I have so much work on here. I really need to get to it." He called repair companies trying to get assistance over the phone. No luck. He called the manufacturer for help. Nothing.

The company had a computer specialist who came by weekly to maintain our system.

Someone said, "Just let the IT guy handle it."

"He won't be back until Monday. I need to get this thing working so I can finish what I started." He punched at the keyboard. After hours of failed attempts, he relented and gave the laptop to the IT guy.

Problem solved. Turns out, while on company time, this idiot was cruising for both women and men. A site he visited launched a virus that seized the laptop's functionality. Cold busted! Playing this oh-I'm-so-busy-working game while trying to screw whomever he could find. He was burnt toast.

The owner confronted him. "How could you do this to me after all I've done for you? I gave you a job with a decent salary, a personal loan, and all kinds of responsibilities. And this is how you repay me? Take your stuff and get out of here."

While everyone else was breaking into sweat trying to keep our jobs, he lived his best life at our expense. He took the long walk of shame. No one made eye contact with him and only a couple people said goodbye. Caught stealing from the company and disloyal to his wife and children. SMH.

A couple days before I left the company, a bunch of us were outside chit-chatting during lunch.

The owner pulled me aside. "Can you please think about staying?"

"Boss, you flatter me, but I've already accepted another job. I had to move on because I cannot afford to be unemployed."

"Darn it. I knew I should've let everybody go and keep you."

I realized that he had to do what was best for the company but not like that. It didn't feel right to me to take a cut in pay or lose my job. I didn't want to take the hit without a promised return when the situation improved. Most people develop an emotional attachment when they've been employed for a while. They tend to lead with their hearts versus thinking with their brains. Whereas, most owners and successful managers operate using logic, problem solving, and critical thinking.

Within two weeks, the five-person sales team was eliminated. Although we were a dysfunctional family, we added value to the company. My goal is to leave a place better than I found it. I felt good walking out the door because I definitely did that.

Chicken Strudel

Serves 8

At this point in my career, perpetual travel was the norm. I committed to visiting my Detroit family at least once a quarter. Chicken strudel was one of the first dishes I prepared for them to demonstrate my cooking skills. They request it on almost every visit. When my schedule allows, I prepare it with roasted root vegetables. Cooking for my family is the highest compliment I can pay my mom. This dish is my tribute to her.

Note: Chicken and sauce can be made a day in advance.

Chicken
1 3-3½ pound whole chicken fryer
1 medium onion, large dice
2 medium carrots, large dice
2 stalks celery, large dice
6 bay leaves

Place chicken, vegetables, and bay leaves in a large pot. Cover with water to 2 inches above ingredients. Bring to a boil, reduce to a simmer, skim off scum, cover with a lid. Cook until chicken is completely cooked (about 35-40 minutes). Remove chicken and cool.

Sauce
½ pound butter, melted

½ cup flour
1 cup heavy cream
Salt and pepper to taste

Strain broth into a medium pot, removing cooked vegetables and bay leaves. Bring broth to a boil and reduce by a third. Blend ½ pound of melted butter with flour to create roux. Thicken broth with roux, add heavy cream, and cook for at least 20 minutes. When finished, the sauce should be a thick consistency. Strain, season to taste with salt and pepper, and cool. Pull chicken meat. Mix with sauce, season to taste, and reserve.

Strudel
4 oz. melted butter
1 box phyllo dough
4 oz. bread crumbs
Egg wash
    1 egg
    ¼ cup water or milk
1 oz. grated or shredded parmesan cheese

Preheat oven to 400°F.

Melt butter. Lay out 1 sheet of phyllo dough and brush with butter. Repeat the process for two more layers. Top the third layer with bread crumbs. For the next two layers of phyllo dough, brush on butter and add bread crumbs. For the sixth and final layer, only butter. Take ½ the filling, shape into a loaf and set on dough. Fold in both sides of dough and roll up from bottom until strudel is complete. Place on baking pan with the strudel seam on the bottom. Brush with egg wash and top with cheese. Bake in preheated oven for 15-20 minutes or until golden.

Note: This recipe makes enough filling for two strudels, each serving 4. The dish is excellent with a green salad and hollandaise sauce.

Win or Learn, but Never Quit

I moved to my new job without fanfare or accolades. This company provided a variety of food products for distributors and end-users. They already had a corporate chef, who worked part-time for years, so I was assigned as a product specialist. I had to learn the entire operation but settled into processing orders. It wasn't sexy or glamorous, but it was honest and necessary work. The company environment was awesome. Everyone got along, respected one another, and performed respective responsibilities. They offered assistance when needed. A full 180° from the previous company. I didn't want to let down the owner, so I worked harder on this job than any other.

When you start a new job, the existing employees try to size you up to see what you're about. My goal was to get through this forming-storming-norming process to get to performing. I think I walked in as the "golden child" because the owner hand-picked me when they didn't need another employee. I minimized my learning curve, jumped in with both feet, and became a trusted member of the staff.

The company was part of a larger network that operated in over thirty states. Each location had an owner and, in some cases, operated as an independent business. For years, the parent company provided a vast array of products to other companies and placed our food products in the company's packaging. This strategy is called private labeling. Great for business but bad for establishing your own brand. Since the company was moving away from the private labeling business, the owner hired me to re-establish the brand and grow market share. How? By developing a TV show.

I wanted to jump and scream, but I kept it together. He involved me in his long-term vision, which had to be presented to the owner of the parent company for funding.

It was the end of the first quarter by the time I learned my purpose. We got down to business to breathe new life into the company as I found ways to add value.

He planned to introduce me to the owner and the partners at an industry convention. Standard operating procedure was to contract catering services for the annual party; however, this year, he wanted his chef and me to work with the catering team. We were to plan the menu, incorporating as much of our products as possible. The chef and I were very excited to bring this first-of-its-kind experience together. This tremendous opportunity would make us and the boss shine.

With no prior model, we started from scratch. About six months in advance, we planned to accommodate 500-600 people. This event would be the talk of the company for the next year, good or bad.

In the meantime, my boss had convinced the corporate owner to entertain the idea of us having a show. He told me to write a proposal using realistic numbers and a little padding for the unexpected.

I worked with my production partner for a month to design a program that accommodated wholesale and retail products. Shifting from chef to producer was quite an accomplishment.

My boss loved the presentation and shared it with the corporate office. Two weeks later, the answer was "no."

I was crushed. *Will I ever realize my dream of having my own show?*

The rejection came a couple of months before the convention. In the back of my mind, I hoped to meet the corporate owner to sell him on the idea. I never mentioned my intentions because my focus was catering the company party.

The three-day Orlando, FL convention consisted of multiple activities including a food show. Scattered evening events were hosted by companies in appreciation of customers and suppliers.

The party that chef and I managed was a huge hit. A few franchise owners hated us, which I attribute to jealousy. Sadly, I didn't have time to approach the owner because he was in high demand.

Since each franchisee worked closely with their own chef, the other food-service teams had no loyalty to me. Their angst was selfish because the menu chef and I organized and executed would have benefited everyone. While I tried to move my agenda forward, they beat down our team for excluding their respective chefs from the project. The internal dissension halted my great idea. Another project DOA, dead on arrival.

The flight back to Colorado was long. We returned to the middle of our busy season. Work boomed. For about two months, we had consistent, steady production that included overtime hours for most of the staff.

My boss called me into his office. I assumed he wanted to discuss a day-to-day matter.

"Keith, I'm sorry, but I'm going to have to let you go. You're a fantastic employee, and the job you did was exceptional. I couldn't have asked for more. But when the owner didn't want to pursue the show, I couldn't justify your position any longer." He handed me an unmarked envelope. "Here's two months of severance. I'm sorry things didn't work out."

I enjoyed my job and the team. I took the news with a smile and strong handshake.

Back on the hamster wheel. Do I look for a job or go back to freelance work? When I was self-employed, I always had opportunities in the pipeline; however, gainful employment took that cushion off the table.

Because I did lots of work on the show idea, I counted the blessing as advancing my celebrity chef brand. But with this setback, I needed to alter my focus. I considered changing my lifestyle to offset this adversity, but God....

The company that let me go a year earlier was under new management. The owner called to see if I was interested in coming back. Absolutely!

I eased back into the new/old company. The hater was still in the building; however, experience prepared me to meet the challenge head-on. The owner wanted to grow his business in a distinct way and was thrilled to have me back. I was thrilled to be there.

With a new production crew and a couple of new office employees, I had to build a powerful, effective, and efficient team. Success. In thirty days, we hit our groove and flowed seamlessly for about fourteen months. Sales and production efficiency escalated to heights never before experienced. The owner contributed by increasing the advertising budget because we needed media to get our message to the public. I traveled the country working for the company and squeezing in time to build my dream.

Our great success was not reflected in the numbers because the owner made "gut" decisions as opposed to assessing the numerical data. To rectify the issue, he hired a team of business advisors to help make critical decisions.

The transition took time because he wanted them to greenlight his ideas, not access their validity.

The day-to-day decisions were managed by a production employee, an office employee, and me. We checked in with the owner and hater on an as-needed basis. For a brief time, we even had the hater on board. Our three-man team never missed a day. We had lots in common including mellow personalities until pushed too far.

Marcus Lemonis of the MSNBC show, *The Profit*, evaluates businesses for strengths and weaknesses regarding product, processes, and people. We had deficits in each category.

- Product: Because our product was extremely perishable, we carried zero inventory.
- Processes: Production was labor intensive. Order fulfillment and delivery were complex systems.
- People: New, inexperienced crew. Volatile, hostile employees like the hater.

Mixed with hate and scenarios from customers, we navigated the minefield. The wonder trio worked up to eighty hours a week. In difficult times, we offered each other support.

With our combined efforts, the company more than doubled. The owner didn't care. He believed my colleagues were trying to sabotage the company's reputation. He spent six months making a case to terminate them.

To minimize HR risks, he hired a consultant and lab technician. His reasoning to us: the consultant was helping him develop a better business plan and work environment, while the lab tech was to implement in-house product testing. He implemented the *Brubaker* move. In the 1980 movie, Robert Redford went undercover as a prisoner to experience the inner workings of the institution. As chaos erupted, he revealed that he was the new warden. Needless to say, everyone was shocked.

All the management staff had to schedule one-on-one time with the consultant to share concerns. The information would be compiled and discussed with the owner. I saw change on the horizon.

The workplace became hostile as the charade caused anxiety, animosity, and anticipation. The owner called a mandatory company meeting. He announced that the newly hired consultant was promoted to general manager (GM). I had hoped to have that position and the correlating compensation. Despite the growth I created for the company, I hadn't had a raise.

The new GM was a wonderful person and tremendous asset to the company. I respectfully moved away from the GM functions I had been performing and supported her wholeheartedly. I used the newfound time to grow my business and build my brand.

As for the lab tech fiasco, the boss's temper caused a disruption in production when he openly chastised a senior employee. The poor employee tried to explain his actions, which only served to upset the boss. He yelled and screamed, making sure the employee—and everyone else—knew who was in charge. The company had a pretty cool policy: if anyone wanted to quit, they could take advantage of a twenty-four hour "cool off" without risk of affecting employment.

After his explosion, the boss said, "You're done! Go up front and wait for me."

"No problem." He left for the office.

The rest of the staff was shocked.

The boss spoke to another employee and directed him to the front office.

Later, we learned that the guy looked at him wrong, so he was escorted out of the facility. We lost two senior production employees who were good at their jobs.

The boss turned his attention to the production manager, a member of my trifecta team. "I want to see you in my office in the morning."

The next day, the GM and production manager waited for the owner to get to work. Once he arrived, he made them wait another forty minutes.

When he finally showed up for the meeting, it was quick and concise. "I'm letting you go."

Without query, the manager got up and left. He anticipated termination when the "lab tech" arrived and had an exit strategy in place. Too many cooks spoil the soup. Domino one down.

His buddy, the IT guy, was livid. He was ready to quit on the spot; however, he calculated the outcomes and took his time implementing them.

I helped the production manager and IT guy land new jobs. They're working with a friend of mine who owns a successful appliance business. They are happy and comfortable being part of a team that treats employees like family. I envy them.

As uncertainty and inner turmoil unfolded, GOD blessed me with four television projects. One project had a small budget but resulted in great relationships. The show was fantastic, but the way we did it was even more special. I picked up so much experience and confidence, which paid dividends long after the project. Like TV, the food industry requires confidence and consistency.

The production company was new, so the owner focused on establishing himself. Because he was so talented, his customer base grew fast. Within a year, he had too much work and had to turn away business. Fantastic for him, but instant death for me. Our little project got pushed to the back burner and, eventually, off the stove.

Although I worked on his project without pay, I refused to ask him to help build my dream unless I could pay him. In good conscience, I couldn't ask him to walk away from paying clients to do me a favor. Our time together was short and sweet, but I expect that we will work together again.

Another project was managed by a firm with about a dozen employees. Because each team member had specific skill sets, they operated in several areas of media production. Their idea was to give me a small recurring role in an existing show and then spin off my own show. They agreed to develop one of my show ideas. Since they were well-established, their focus was growth into other segments, some outside of traditional media. With a company like that, I was just another cookie in the jar. They had so many fish to fry that my vision marinated indefinitely.

From time-to-time, we developed strategies on how to proceed. But then business got in the way, and they fell off the map. I sent show ideas, scripts, and treatments but got nothing in return. I wanted to run with my vision; however, I needed to work through the process: crawl, walk, and then run. Their sense of urgency did not align with mine. We had tremendous opportunities with plenty of low-hanging fruit. All we had to do was grab it. Disappointed.

We executed our plan, but it was painfully slow. The project stretched for well over two years, standard for them. Lots of talking, little action. While we discussed, strategized, and planned, a host of companies cranked out content. I had too much invested and changed my mindset to stick with them no matter what. I had to get something tangible from the collaboration, so I rode with them simmering over low heat.

Since I didn't have disposable income to invest, I got involved with start-up companies. Although seldom monetary, I extract something from every project. I use the experience to critique myself and look for opportunities to improve. I worked and adjusted as needed. I surrounded myself with people who saw what I saw.

It didn't take long for the next opportunity to come knocking. A very good friend was an instructor at a couple of universities. From time to time, he asked me to speak to one of his classes. After one session, a couple of students said that they were impressed with my presentation and wanted to work with me.

One student said, "You better be ready to work hard because I've always wanted to do a cooking show. I'll work you into the ground."

I chuckled. *You're going to work* **me** *into the ground?* "Let's do it."

The work I did with the student was a blast, and our first project was memorable. He assembled an amazing team. I assumed that his team would be peers, but boy was I wrong. He curated a powerful group of seasoned veterans. I was shocked.

As they set up, we had casual conversations, which relaxed me. The student served as the director and lead cameraman.

In the middle of the first take, the director said, "Cut! Keith, I need to talk to you."

The crew checked their equipment.

"I need you to tone it down."

"Tone it down?"

"Yeah, you know. Be a bit more reserved."

Confused, I shrugged and looked at the crew.

A member of the film crew said, "Hey. I think you're wrong. He's doing fine."

All the validation I needed to speak up. "I already toned down my delivery from how I usually do it. You want me to go softer?"

He nodded.

Before the next take, I played around with a few delivery styles almost making light of his request. The crew got into it, and we had a little fun.

That impromptu exercise changed the atmosphere. When we started back, the magic took the project to another level. We cranked out impressive content. Between takes, I talked to the pros. They shared that they had no idea what they were getting into when they signed on for the project. However, after working with me, they said that it was one of the best things they had done in years. Dare I say, "Well done!"

When we wrapped the first part of the project, I was anxious to see the edit. Following a shoot, I want to see the results ASAP. For this project, I wanted to help select the footage that was going on the screen.

The student director said, "Thanks, but no thanks."

It took over a year for him to edit one segment. No matter how I tried, I couldn't get him to go faster. I'll never understand how someone can invest all this effort and not have anything to show for it. We got busy with other projects and went our separate ways until he referred me for another project.

"Hey, Keith. I'm the cameraman on a project with a larger production company."

"Okay."

He told me about the team of specialized experts and the project.

Intrigued, I called and left a message. "I know I'm late to the process. But if your chef doesn't show and you need a replacement, please let me know. I'd love to help out." I stewed for about ten minutes for the late notice.

The other group called. "You're not too late. We didn't have anyone selected for the chef's role. If you're still interested, the job is yours. We can meet to discuss the specifics, but it has to be soon. The project is moving along fast."

"Absolutely. Let me know what works for you and I'm there."

The producer, director, and talent coordinator explained what they were trying to accomplish. I learned that the pros from the other project were on this project as well. They put in a good word for me.

When I showed up at the first shoot, they had over $100,000 worth of equipment. This team didn't need motivation from me. They had their own goals and dreams, and better yet, they were serious about achieving them.

The scope of the project was pretty cool. I was blown away with all the progress they had made. Since we filmed in the director's backyard, they decided to hold several rehearsals over four months to work out the bugs. The yard was massive. He converted it into three different sets: a sandy beach, an amphitheater, and an outdoor restaurant.

The final taping, scheduled to stream live, would serve as the pilot. Because it's still in development, I cannot share more details on the concept. Look for it on TV someday soon.

My part was simple: make a dish and hit talking points. Once edited, I would have about three minutes of the screen for a 60-minute show.

For the first rehearsal, the behind-the-scenes crew arrived well ahead of the talent. My call time was 3:00 PM; however, I arrived at 10:00 AM to make sure I was good. It took several hours to prep for the three-minute, backyard-barbecue segment. I cut, marinated, and grilled chicken, grilled vegetables and made coleslaw.

Surrounded by that much talent, I didn't want to be the weakest link by messing up or causing delays. Just thinking about it made me nervous. I finished my prep work by early afternoon and then practiced. After rehearsing the soft script a few times, I asked the producer if I could make some minor changes. He encouraged me to write my own lines.

The anticipation was fun and unbearable. The producer and director spoke to everyone, dialing in the last-minute details. When showtime arrived, Mother Nature gifted us with a half-hour rain and windstorm. Did I mention that the show was filmed outside?

I felt sorry for the technicians because much of their equipment was tossed around. The producer and director surveyed the damage, making adjustments to salvage the day. They developed and executed a contingency plan. The true definition of weathering the storm.

The technicians put everything back together despite a few minor issues. The talent, on the other hand, had all kinds of issues. Since this job was pro bono, most of them had other commitments. They bailed. The managers were determined to get content out of this, so they pushed and pleaded for people to stay.

With most of the talent leaving, I played a more significant role: I opened the show.

They were so impressed with my performance that they modified the show to include me as the host. Awesome. I went from a last-minute addition to hosting. God is good! Even with all the issues, the shoot went well. I killed my cooking segment and hosting responsibilities.

Many of the people asked if I was a "real chef" or talent.

"You're far too kind. I'm a 'real chef' who aspires to do TV."

"Wow. You're really good. You could have a show on the Food Network."

"Thank you. I wish it were that easy."

We captured excellent content and had fun doing it. The schedule had us wrapping late evening, but we didn't leave until midnight. I didn't care because a major hurdle was accomplished. I was on their radar.

The producer said, "Keith, thanks for hanging in and doing such a great job."

"My pleasure."

"The next shoot is in three weeks. You available?"

"Absolutely."

I floated on cloud nine during the drive home. Thrilled about the possibilities, I replayed the evening. My forty-five-minute drive seemed like a minute. I only remember starting the car and parking in the driveway. I guess the car was on autopilot.

A few days later, I received a partial edit of the show by email. I didn't have to chase, beg, or motivate them to do anything. Two days later, they sent another email with links to a sizzle reel and an edited version of the full episode. Awesome delivery time and amazing content.

They called to see if I had watched. They wanted to add a female hostess to work with me on the next shoot and asked what else could be done differently. Working with pros was refreshing. I appreciated them including me in the decision-making process.

They hired a local actress who was great at her craft. We were supposed to spend time together prior to the shoot to develop on-screen chemistry. For various reasons, the only time we had was a few hours before the shoot.

They gave her the primary hosting duties. Although I was disappointed, I did my best to complement her. I killed it.

After quick-turnaround editing, they called me.

"Keith, you shine. The hostess doesn't play well with you, so we're going in another direction. We need to find someone who matches your intensity and energy."

They held open auditions and asked me to read with potential candidates. It was an amazing experience to read lines and roleplay with talent: actresses and comediennes.

It took a couple of days to select the best candidate. As before, they wanted us to connect to develop on-screen chemistry prior to shooting. My co-host was a local comedian who had jobs booked across the country. Between our hectic schedules, we could not confirm a pre-shoot meeting.

We arrived early the day of the shoot. Her comedic improvisation was just what the producer wanted. I didn't want to lose my position, so I thought about how I could be funny to keep pace with the professional. Out of my element, but I wasn't about to come up short.

When it was go-time, she struggled. I'm sure they expected her to ad-lib, but she just couldn't do it. Timing and delivery were off. Her comfortability increased as filming progressed, and we got good footage.

The guys put a rush on the edit. Anxious to see the cutting-room magic, I clicked the link. She was edited out of the entire segment.

They showed the episode to several of their industry friends. The general consensus was that the show was good, but it might not have a large audience appeal. If they wanted to sell it nationwide, changes were necessary. The management team adjusted the show as recommended.

Do they still have a position for me?

Yes, they did. And it was prominent.

They recruited a couple of folks to help bring the new show to life. They came to the project full of TV experience, having a string of successful shows airing on several networks. Their success formula was executed eerily similar to how I create recipes. Add a little of this, take out all of that. Sprinkle in these three things and there you have it.

We met twice a month for six months to flesh out ideas and develop the show. I wanted to keep the new show as close as possible to the old one because the genuineness made it unique. We went from making the show for ourselves to making it for profit. As a result, we lost our creativity and power.

It was fascinating to experience how a real show is developed, but I knew that this was the beginning of the end. Without much enthusiasm, we put the show concept together, which lives in an incubator waiting to be brought to life. The only things we have to show for our efforts are the original edits, knowledge gained, new friendships, and memories.

From time to time, I check in with the director and producer for an update.

"Don't give up hope, Keith. Eventually, we'll carve out time to make it happen."

Since I had more eggs in the basket, I devoted time to other projects.

Every year, a local production company solicited ideas for TV shows. The submission process was simple. Create a one-to-five-minute video trailer and include a signed treatment, which explains the show idea. All major networks require you to sign away your rights.

When I found out about the opportunity, the submission deadline was in one week. Three of those days were booked, so I had four days to create a piece. Because I developed and nurtured relationships throughout my career, I made a call and assembled a team. We turned out a video with a day to spare.

The production company factored in two months to review submissions. Instead of twiddling my thumbs, I pursued another one of my ideas.

Like clockwork, when one project closed, another one opened. My next project was another show pilot with a significant partner who had skin in the game. This show was set up to go from the internet to TV once we got enough content in the queue.

I had two other aspects of my empire that needed attention: public speaking and appearances. So much to do, so little time. I was hopeful that when the show—any show—hit the airwaves, everything else would fall in line.

Years prior, the brilliant IT guy I met in Denver, J.R., mentioned that he would build me a website to use as a calling card. The online presence would also attract potential companies to his web design capabilities.

He said, "I'm not going to use a template. I'll build it from code."

He might as well have been speaking Spanish to me. "Whatever you want to do is fine. You're the expert."

After launching my website, ChefKDJ.com, he signed over fifty clients. He walked away from his job and opened a business without much growing pains.

He kept my site up-to-date and stayed on me to provide him with content. I was blessed to work with him. His clientele grew, and while I wasn't generating revenue from the site, my brand expanded. The reciprocal relationship generated mutual benefits.

While out of town, I called him to discuss another opportunity. The call went to voicemail. Once I returned home, I learned that he was in the hospital. I visited him right away.

With his wife by his side, he said, "Keith, I'm dying."

"What are you talking about, J.R.? You'll be better in no time." I did my best to encourage him. "With technology and advancements in science, surely something can be done. You have options. Don't be discouraged. Let's figure this thing out."

"I have hepatitis C. I need a new liver."

"Wow. Okay, so you're on the donor list, right?"

"Yes. I've been on the list for a while." He sighed. "But because of my background, it's unlikely that I'll receive a transplant."

"Background? What are you talking about?"

"Well, I went to prison, so I'm an afterthought to society."

I knew that he went to jail, but I didn't know that incarceration affected his ability to receive an organ. While I tried to process the news, he hit me with another bombshell.

"I don't have much time left. I don't want to be a financial burden to my wife," he smiled at her, "so I'm going home to die."

"Wait! What? It isn't over. Come on, man, let's figure this thing out and put together some options."

"Don't bother. I already called hospice. They'll be here later today to take me home."

Crushed. I cleared my schedule to be with him as much as I could.

When the hospice folks arrived to put his affairs in order, I went to the cafeteria. I racked my brain for answers. I returned to his room with nothing but a heavy heart.

We sat in silence for about ten minutes. If he were rich, he'd have options.

He had a hushed conversation with his wife as I wept on the inside, trying not to make any noise. I didn't want him to hear me break down. I didn't want to add to his pain.

Hospice took him home in an ambulance. I helped the delivery crew set up his area with an adjustable bed.

A nurse arrived. Muscular with hair past his butt, arm tattoos, and a thick goatee, I estimated his age as mid to late fifties. He looked more like a member of a biker gang than a nurse. In contrast to his appearance, he was very compassionate. He got J.R.'s vitals, administered medicine, and took the extra time to have a pleasant conversation, which helped my friend relax.

I listened to the powerful story my dying friend told.

He used to be a cop with the Hawaii police. One day, after his shift, he and his partner stopped at a hole-in-the-wall bar. They stayed for a few hours, kicking back and having a good time with some locals. I'm sure the drinks were plenty, and the conversation escalated with bravado throughout the night.

The next day, his supervisor called him into his office. DEA agents wanted to question him about a guy he talked to at the bar the previous night.

The guy of interest was one of the largest drug dealers in Asia. They had him surveilled for quite some time. Following a quick investigation, J.R. was cleared. The DEA wanted him and his partner to go undercover and pursue a relationship with the dealer. After much consternation, they agreed to get illegal drugs off the streets and put bad guys in jail.

Both skilled officers, they were valuable assets to the team. They flew all over Hawaii and Asia participating in illegal activities, while gathering information to build cases.

They were point men on several drug deals. One, in particular, took place in the middle of field in Vietnam. As the exchange was made, bullets started flying. Several people were shot and a few, including his partner, killed.

J.R. was shot just above his left eye. One of his crew helped him to a car. Because he was losing so much blood, they stopped at a clinic on the side of the road. In the middle of nowhere, and with little equipment, the staff did what they could to patch him up. The blood they used to save his life was infected with hepatitis C.

After he recovered, he went rogue to track down the person responsible for his partner's death. He caught and killed him in Colorado, which led to his conviction. While serving his sentence, he learned that he had the disease.

He was added to the bottom of the donor list. Flagged as a ward of the state, he had little chance of receiving a liver.

To survive, he reinvented himself. He chose computers as his ticket and took the IT job at the equipment representative group where I met him.

After years of anticipating death, he died at home in two weeks. What a waste. He was a great man who paid more than his debt to society and built a respectable life.

Three days after he passed, his dog died. His wife believed that they were otherworldly connected. She had them cremated and kept their ashes on the mantle.

Left alone, I sympathized with his wife. I helped move out the hospice donation and prepared food for the wake.

With a pre-existing condition, he wasn't eligible for life insurance. She inherited his school loans and mortgage.

I visited her every week until I felt she could function with her grief.

After six months of trying to make ends meet, she decided to sell the house and pay off what she could. To offset the deficit, she filed bankruptcy. She tried to keep his business going, but it became too much. She moved back to Wisconsin to assist her aging parents.

Outside of my memories, the only thing I had from him was the website. I kept it as he built it for about two years as a silent memorial to him. My takeaway was that life is precious. You never know what tomorrow will bring, so the choice is simple: get busy living or get busy dying.

My healing took time. As I understood life more clearly, my priorities shifted; I became more sensitive. I knew that each success and failure had embedded lessons. I just needed to be open to receive it.

With my newfound clarity, I needed to address the hole in my foundation: my website. I searched for someone to update it; however, most of them could not write code. I held onto the site J.R. created for as long as I could.

With the social media explosion, I had to move forward. One of the people I hired for Honey Smoked Fish Company, Joey, had the skills to recreate my site. Everything my friend did is gone.

I often look at my website and reminisce about my friend. It energizes and helps me focus.

I moved away from chef, salesman and building my own brand to what the company needed—an official brand ambassador. The goal was to grow the company brand to national prominence. We didn't have funds for nationwide radio and TV commercials, so our grass-root efforts were word of mouth and local advertising.

The owner tried to be the in-front-of-the-camera talent for commercials, but he walked away from it and designated me as the face of the company.

I promoted across the state. Interviews, video content, and events: concerts, food shows, and more. I conducted cooking demos, passed out samples, and spoke to the public to build our brand.

Stretched thin, but thrilled with the opportunities, the on-the-job training was a game changer. The upside to being the face of a company was that people recognized me.

"Are you the guy on the commercials?"

"Wait a minute. I recognize you. Aren't you the guy I saw on TV?"

"Excuse me. Would it be okay if I took a picture with you?"

When it came to radio, people recognized my voice.

"I heard you on the radio today."

"You have a distinct voice. I'd recognize it anywhere."

"You're the guy who talks about food and recipes on the radio. You have a nice accent. Where are you from?"

I loved it.

Another benefit is the relationships I've developed with celebrities, sports figures, and politicians. The brand ambassador position came at the right time. Mutually beneficial, it helped me grow personally and professionally. It provided me a glimpse into what the world of celebrity could become. Look at God's irony.

I'm taking a new chef's position at a local appliance store. My role is delivering a culinary program to existing customers and business partners. I'm not stepping into a position but rather building it from scratch. I can easily work sixty hours a week for the job and twenty on my brand. The grind continues.

"Hi, I'm Keith, and I'm a workaholic."

Blackened Salmon with Amaretto Orange Butter Sauce

Serves 4

Live stage cooking demonstrations are essential for branding. As a huge seafood fan, I incorporate it into my diet and demonstrations, which helps demystify apprehension about properly cooking it. This easy recipe touches all the fun elements of performance cooking: quick, healthy, flaming, and tasty.

Blackening Spice Mixture
1 teaspoon chili powder
1 teaspoon ancho chili powder
1 teaspoon cumin powder
1 teaspoon garlic powder
1 teaspoon onion powder
½ teaspoon paprika
½ teaspoon oregano
½ teaspoon salt
½ teaspoon pepper
¼ teaspoon cayenne

Combine spices.

Salmon
4 6-ounce portions of salmon fillet, skinned and boned
1 ounce butter, melted
1 cup mixed baby lettuce, washed and dried

Pre-heat a cast iron skillet to medium-high. Brush salmon with melted butter and generously coat with blackening spice. Cook salmon, seasoned side down, about 3-5 minutes. Turn over salmon. Finish the cooking until the fillet is done, about 3-5 minutes.

Amaretto Orange Butter Sauce
4 ounces amaretto
1 shallot, minced
2 ounces vegetable stock
2 large oranges, segmented and juiced
2 ounces butter
1 tablespoon fresh parsley, minced
2 tablespoons fresh basil, cut into thin strips (chiffonade)
2 ounces almonds, toasted
Kosher salt to season to taste

In another pan, start the sauce by flaming off the alcohol from the amaretto. Once the flame goes out, add shallot and vegetable stock. Cook mixture about 1 minute, then add the juice from the oranges. Cook until it reduces about half. Add butter and cook until it melts. Add parsley, basil, and almonds. Adjust seasoning with salt.

Place salmon off center on the baby lettuce. Arrange orange segments decoratively on top of both. Top with sauce. Serve immediately.

Revenge is a Dish Best Served Cold

On my journey to executive chef, I often encountered haters—people who wanted to kill my dream or force me into their version of who I am. Although some people are diminished, defeated, and destroyed by naysayers, I used it as electrifying motivation. I know who I am, and I know my truth. I can be whatever I want, which may not look how others expect. They say that revenge is a dish best served cold. It took me many years to prepare that dish because the best revenge is a life well-lived.

With every triumph and disappointment, I pivoted, changed plans, and kept my eyes on my dreams. I learned, developed new skills, and remained flexible despite my rigidity and impatience. I sacrificed and occasionally refused to compromise. I made decisions to take care of my family.

I now understand that the process is the true journey. Don't be so consumed with the goal—and its pursuit—that you lose appreciation for the process. That's where growth, maturity, and improvement happen.

Am I still a workaholic? Yes. While experience and age may cause me to slow down, I will use my energy to work toward my goals.

I packed more than my belongings when I left Detroit for Denver. I packed ambition, belief in myself, and the hope that I could live a better life. I thank Detroit for equipping me with the fortitude to survive. Who knew that by saying "yes" to Denver, I was saying "yes" to a world of opportunities? God knew.

Detroit. I love my city. Hearing the name brings excitement and anticipation. Like the oxygen in the blood pumping through my veins, I take her with me everywhere. She'll contribute her unique perspective to whatever the situation. With heartfelt love, I trust her. She trusts me and has never let me down.

Fried Shrimp with Watermelon and Jicama Coleslaw

Serves 4

I created this recipe early in my career as my go-to dish for a lasting impression. Although it's not the healthiest meal because of the fried shrimp, I balanced it with coleslaw. Total umami—the sum of the whole is greater than the individual parts.

Shrimp

12 shrimp (sized at 16/20 shrimp per pound), peeled and deveined
¼ cup flour
Salt
White pepper
Egg wash
    1 egg
    ¼ cup water or milk
1 cup breadcrumbs
2 cups peanut or vegetable oil for deep-frying

Season flour with salt and white pepper. Do a standard breading procedure with the shrimp (flour, egg wash, and breadcrumbs). Refrigerate for at least 2 hours.

Pre-heat oil to 350°F for frying. Place shrimp in oil and cook until golden. Remove from oil, drain, and serve with slaw.

Watermelon and Jicama Coleslaw

2 cups watermelon, julienne with no seeds
2 cups jicama, julienne
1 medium-size poblano or green pasilla pepper, julienne with no seeds
1 small jalapeño pepper, julienne with no seeds
¼ cup olive oil
8 thin scallions, thinly sliced
¾ cup fresh cilantro, chopped fine
Juice of 2 limes
Salt and pepper to taste

Place all ingredients into a bowl and toss together until incorporated. Season to taste with salt and pepper and serve with fried shrimp.

About the Author

Under the tutelage of the consummate Master Chef Edward Janos, Keith Denard Jones jumpstarted his culinary career spanning more than forty years. As a certified executive chef, and former member of Chaîne des Rôtisseurs, he mastered execution and excellence. Whether preparing signature cuisine, conducting cooking demonstrations, or consulting restaurateurs on creative marketing ideas, his knowledge, wisdom, and professionalism speak for themselves.

Having overcome poverty and oral cancer, Chef Keith mentors youth and serves the homeless. A natural at inspiring others to become the best version of themselves, he understands that the journey to achieve a goal is just as important—if not more than—accomplishing it. In addition to his debut book, *Cooking Up Your Dreams*, Chef Keith's sophomore project, *Well Done*, chronicles highlights of his culinary journey and lessons learned along the way.

With career milestones like sharing the stage with Tom Hanks, being featured on an episode of *Bar Rescue* with Jon Taffer, and participating in Michelle Obama's Chefs Move to Schools program, Chef Keith's culinary genius has created numerous opportunities. From brand ambassador for Honey Smoked Fish Company to creating custom cuisine for stellar events, he understands that his flavor is only possible through God's favor.

For a private-chef experience, speaking engagements, and bulk purchases, contact Chef Keith at ChefKDJ.com, TheWellDoneBook.com, or keith@chefkdj.com.

About Queen V Publishing

The Doorway to

YOUR Destiny!

Go thou and publish abroad the kingdom of God.

—Luke 9:60 ESV

Committed to transforming manuscripts into polished works of art, **Queen V Publishing** is a company of standard and integrity. We offer an alternative that allows the message in YOU to do what it was sent to do for OTHERS.

QueenVPublishing.com

Serving professional speakers and experts to magnify and monetize their message by publishing quality books

Acknowledgments

I mistakenly thought that one of the hardest things I'd ever do was participate in a culinary competition for the chance to win a medal. Writing a book far eclipses that, challenging me in ways I never imagined. However, upon completion, it is far more gratifying than I can express. Being that it was so emotionally exhaustive, I'm not sure I will ever travel down this path again (I need time to recover). So I must thank the people who supported me to make the idea floating around in my mind into a published book.

Everything begins and ends with family. I know everyone thinks theirs is the absolute best, and I'm no different.

My wife, Martha, my rock! You support me with whatever I need to achieve my goals. You never criticize or discourage, only smile and reassure me to do what must be done. I will always have your back. You are the ying to my yang.

To my children, I'm so proud of the adults you've become. Every parent wants their children to live happy and make this world a better place. You exceeded my expectations. I love you more than words can convey.

Dicia, my beautiful daughter, inside and out. You've grown into a spectacular woman. You are blessed with the most beautiful spirit of anyone I know. A young matriarch, humane, knowledgeable, poised, and wise beyond your years.

Nini, my beautiful daughter, inside and out. You've been by my side since day one and never wavered. You always trusted and believed in me. You left home to create your own way and never looked back—determined, committed, and strong.

Zac, my handsome son, inside and out. Independent, smart, compassionate, and strong-willed. With eagerness and courage, you walked your own path determined to be your own man. You're so much more composed than I was at your age. I anxiously await all the wonderful achievements yet to be seen.

Ma, everything I have accomplished—and yet to achieve—is directly connected to you. Your unconditional love, support, and encouragement formed the rock-solid foundation that I stood on to build my life. Thank you for giving me exactly what I needed.

Gret, no one has a better sister. You're the most genuine and warm-hearted person I know. You see the beauty in everything. Your first decision is to love and support. You're the glue that keeps our family together and the kind spirit that resonates in all of us.

Rod, you are the best brother…ever! You're the consummate protector and warrior. When Dad checked out on us, you stepped up and unapologetically worked to keep us from harm. You made the ultimate sacrifice for our family. You took the hit for us, and I owe you my life.

Art, my brother from another mother. You called me out of the clear blue and shifted the trajectory of my life in an instant. When I was an unmolded hunk of clay, you constructed your masterpiece, committing to walk with me until our final days. I love you. I am honored to have you as a friend, mentor, and brother.

My friends: Chef Dan, Chef Eddie, Chef Bobby, Chef Alex, Chef Selene, Chef Cynthia, Chef Kimberly, Chef Chris, Ryan, and Will. I value your friendship more than you'll ever know. You helped me grow into a better man. Guidance, support, wisdom, honesty, critique, and compassion are just a few of the things you gave. Genuine and rooted in love, you planted seeds that continue to grow. Friends for life.

Mentors: Duncan, Ed, and Kevin. You are a blessing to me. You came into my life at the precise time I needed you.

You taught me how to be a better man. Not only did you guide me, you loved me.

Duncan, you left too soon, but you have a lasting place in my heart, mind, and spirit.

Bosses: Jim and Kevin. I'm so grateful that you decided to take a chance on me. I appreciate your vision, leadership, and how you execute your plan. I am thrilled to be associated with winners and blessed to be a part of your company.

Editors: Amani, Jodie, Paige, Bridgett, Robin, and Colin. I appreciate your contributions to help get my thoughts together. The journey has been long and tedious but well worth the effort. I learned much in the process and would not have made it without your timely input.

Colin, thanks for designing my dual-perspective author photo.

A special thank you to Jodie, who took me and the book over the top. Your timely, observant, and sharp assessments have me forever indebted.

Publisher - Valerie and her Queen V Publishing team. What a blessing for me to have found you! I'm at a loss for words to pay tribute to you for bringing my manuscript to life. Once your process started, I was blown away. Your professionalism, knowledge, commitment, determination, and more are something to behold. You've taken me to new heights and made me a better writer. No way would I have come anywhere close to the product we produced. I didn't just write a book; we created something of which I'm thoroughly proud—a lasting legacy to my life. PRICELESS.

CPSIA information can be obtained
at www.ICGtesting.com
Printed in the USA
LVHW012341010821
694126LV00012B/791

9 780996 299169